**A Memoir
by Sankalpit Salaria**

THROUGH THE DARKENED GLASS

Published by: Notion Press

Printed in India

Table of Contents

For My Fellow Readers

This book is for those who have been broken, misunderstood, and alone. If you've been in a place that seems impossible to get out of, or if you ever felt that no one can ever understand the pain you are carrying, know that you are not alone.

I've walked through darkness, carried the weight of memories, and wrestled with feelings of abandonment and isolation. But I've also learned that healing is possible and that even in the hardest moments, there is a glimmer of hope.

It's not my story. It is for those who ever had to feel the burden of their own experiences and wonder if they can really go on from there. From these pages, I hope you feel connected like you're in solidarity with me, and maybe you find your way toward healing.

To my Nanu and Nani,

For your overflowing love, profound wisdom, and steadiness. You have always been my foundation, and I never find the words to thank you for all the care you gave me throughout the years.

Nanu, Nani, if you are reading this, stop right there. There are things written here that I doubt will worry you, and I want to stay far away from bothering you. Do not read this; it's for the world to see but not for your or any family member's eyes.

Introduction

In a park filled with positivity and joy, surrounded by beautiful natural greenery, kids playing and their humming, making it feel like a hot shower after a tiring day, why are you sitting alone and quietly on a bench with your head fallen like a prisoner? They ask...

But little did they know this prisoner had multiple complaints of terrorising the peace of mind of an individual against himself who himself judged him guilty of his crimes and sentenced him guilty of his crimes against himself and sentenced him to spend a long, long, long time in prison with himself.

But 'individual'?

Who?!

This is the story of many individuals these days who have suffered through many issues and problems. The interesting part is that the majority of them no longer identify their major problems as problems anymore because it has become such a norm for them, as in the frequency of happening that particular event is quite high in their lives or no one listened to them when they opened up about their problems or maybe they never felt like they deserve the help or in the majority of the cases this all in all together. Well, this is how the majority of teens have been treated in desi households.

It's funny that Desi people often take pride in their strong cultural emphasis on joint families, which are believed to offer individuals a richer social life.

Large joint families are thought to provide children with a better upbringing, as they have the privilege of receiving attention from a wide network of family members. This, in turn, is believed to contribute to the overall growth and well-being of the children. At the same time, one in every fourth kid is depressed due to either child abuse or pressure put up by parents and by not treating them right. And if you are reading this, there is a high chance that you are one of the fourth ones...(the depressed one!!!)

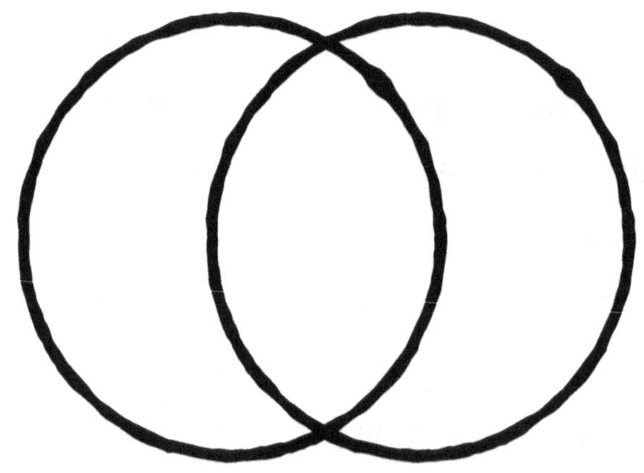

CHAPTER ONE

Us

Family - a word that often conveys comfort, care, and safety, but that's not the case for us, or I should say the majority of desi teenagers. The walls of our houses are thick with secrets, and silence is spoken louder than words.

Love has become conditional, only earned by either good grades or maybe sometimes guests visit you, so the sweet, happy and caring family mask is on until they also start speaking harshly about you. And warmth?! That's a rare currency.

I learned early how trust could be broken as easily as the promises whispered in the dark.

How, behind closed doors, does this persona of a happy family begin to crack? Well, the persona isn't the only thing that cracks, but I do, too... we do, we all do.

Those cracks and fissures in our self-perception often serve as the main source of our low self-esteem, leading to a lack of confidence in many aspects of our lives. Leaving us quiet and unspeakable in many instances, or we find not speaking the best option in many situations.

Well, not speaking is right in some cases, but not in every case. Silence is one thing that is taught behind those closed doors quite religiously, regardless of one's current circumstances, if one wins, they teach him how he won because he only listened to his parents and he should continue doing so and if it's anything less than a win the whole blame is on the individual for not behaving or performing the task as one was supposed to by his parents and that was the reason why he didn't perform well and expects us to embrace the silence all this time.

Such pointing measures taken by parents turn into a child's painful sores, resulting in hampering an individual's mental and social growth.

The teenage years are when a person learns the most because it is a natural period of growth and learning for humans. During this time, individuals gain valuable experiences and knowledge, and such experiences hamper one's growth a lot.

As a child who's facing all those strict punishments and actions taken by their parents, it gets very traumatic for them to survive that situation while that's happening. The anger and negative gestures displayed towards a child while punishing them can have a significant impact on their emotional well-being.

This type of behaviour has a high chance of causing children to develop trauma or anxiety, which can make it difficult for them to navigate social interactions and relationships later in life. Such experiences can harm children and make it challenging for them to thrive and succeed as they grow and interact with others in society.

There is a high chance the majority of byproducts of such behaviour in kids are reading this book, and you are one of them. Now, you can connect the dots as to why you often get uncomfortable while socialising, and the sudden nervousness catches your nerves.

"I have no home to run back to; I have no soul to speak to, what I all have is

my natural guardian cutting my best friend up through the throat, my best friend, my self-esteem."

Suffering is one thing we all come down to and relate to as kids, as humans who have been suffering through the same for a long time, and we sympathise with each other. We appreciate each other. Or we should, or you should if you don't.

Parents are the ones whom a kid looks up to; they are the natural guardians of their kids. They are the ones who gave us birth, brought us into this beautiful world and took this beautiful job to raise a new soul to fit in this society.

The innocent little soul is completely dependent on them. The soul learns language, behaviour, feelings, and a lot from them and their actions, and eventually, it very obviously gets very attached to them.

The soul shares everything with their parents and learns new things with them with the purest feelings and intentions. And when they turn their backs on their child when they need them the most, it is the first betrayal of that individual's life.

The punishment one receives, and the physical abuse is the result of their action. Is this fair?... Was that little soul deserving of all that?

The physical abuse physically might heal in a week or two, but the mental damage it leads to, along with betrayal and misuse of the position of a natural guardian, might take forever to heal. The dent they leave so casually on one physically is directly proportional to another dent left on one's mind and mental health...

This is the time when children become over-conscious about their actions, words, and feelings and trap themselves in a cage made up of their thoughts and beliefs, which are mostly negative. A psychological trap of believing a vast amount of negative thoughts with a widespread one is...

'No one likes them but just politely tolerates them'

And so has been the case with me... I think I was quite young back then, but young enough to realise that my family wasn't like others.

I often used to visit with my Nani-Nanu and liked spending time with them back when I was a kid, but these days, when I look back at that topic, I realise I just liked spending time outside my house.

The times at home were different: silence filled with terror, thick air, cussing, but taking it as a word of affirmation was the only choice I had and those scary shadows and footsteps of him... I wish I could erase it from my memory.

My house wasn't a place of rest but a place like enemy territory where one single mistake and the very second, you are in big trouble. This has been my training ground, where I learned to be careful of my movement and to watch my tone.

There were moments when it would erupt, filling the room, and I would shrink into myself, wondering what did I do? What went wrong this time? Am I so dumb to even perform a single task given by him?!

And my mother... She was the only thing I had to protect me from him, who used to stand between him and me like a tough mountain, who was protecting me from all those demonic slurs and abuse from that man. But she wasn't there to protect me every time.

Her silence was a comfort at times, but mostly, it made me feel like I was the one who messed up everything every time.

By the time I was a teenager, my mother had pushed me away to a boarding school to keep me away from the very toxic environment of the house, and soon she left too to live with my Nani-Nanu, but little did she know the damage to my mind was already done by then.

Those years shaped me in a way I didn't even understand then. I thought I could handle it; I thought I was strong enough to carry the weight. But as I would later find out, some burdens stay with you long after you have left the house they were built in. Just like that day after school when I came back home, and there was no one to welcome me home... either with lunch or with scary stares...

CHAPTER TWO

The Empty House

I still remember the sound of my shoes hitting the ground that afternoon. A rhythm I knew too well. I had walked the same path home from school so many times before, always dreading what I might find when I opened the front door. Meanwhile, each step pulled me closer to home.

Most days, the walk back from school was a slow, hesitant shuffle, me thinking of the possibilities of what would greet me behind those doors today. Sometimes, it was my father's icy stares or my mother's tired voice telling me to keep quiet, keep out of sight. Other times, it was worse.

But that day, sorting felt off, something was different. The house was eerily quiet, the kind of silence that made my heart race, but not because I feared the usual storm of voices or heavy glares. This time, the absence of everything hit me hardest. It felt like the calm before the storm.

When I reached the front door, I hesitated; my hands were cold, and my feet felt lighter. I had no then what awaited me wasn't the furry or fear that I had grown so used to. I opened the door and walked through the well, the well which always attracted me because of multiple reasons. One of them has been a constant urge to jump in it.

I walked through, and the silence hit me like a wall. It wasn't just the usual quiet, it was deeper, heavier, the kind that seeps into your skin. I took a step inside, and it felt like the house was holding its breath, waiting for something that would never come.

My grandmother's absence hung in the air, and for once, her side of the house seemed as hollow as ours. She lived on the far side of the garden, where the rooms were always bright and spacious, untouched by the struggles that weighed down our corner of this fractured place. She never failed to remind us, with every small act of control, that she held all the power.

Her so-called kindness was always a transaction, even the lunch she gave me every afternoon was laced with a quiet disdain, as if feeding me was a favour rather than a duty.

I stood in the doorway of the kitchen, staring at the empty counter where a plate would have sat, my breath catching in the stagnant air. There was a brutality to the quiet, a sharpness that cut deeper than any words she could have spoken.

It was a silence that bled into everything, seeping into the very marrow of the house and turning it into a monument to neglect. I felt the weight of it pressing down on me, a suffocating emptiness that was somehow heavier than her presence had ever been.

Today, there was no lunch, no scornful glances or sharp words. Just empty countertops and an even emptier house. I walked through our cramped rooms, the air thick with a stillness that felt almost unnatural, as if the house itself had noticed the change.

It wasn't that I missed her presence, it was more like I didn't know what to do with the silence she left behind. The quiet felt raw, like a wound, and in that moment, the house seemed larger than ever, its walls stretching out to swallow me whole.

I got into our room and changed with a weird gesture and environment the room had offered me. The brutality was a thing I've always been exposed to, but this time, it came along with loneliness. Loneliness, a scare of abandonment, the voices from the well, along with all those shadows lurking around the house. I sat on the couch and started waiting for my mother to return home from school.

The time flew fast! It was *3 pm* I reached home, and in the blink of an eye, it was *4 pm* already. I expected my mother to come anytime soon now because she usually returned by that time, but that day, I struggled to find the noise of her scooty across the road by our house between the noises of trucks, cars and bikes.

No one was home!

My heart was rising as the time went by. Since then, a single second started feeling like an intense wait. The air started getting thicker, and the surroundings started getting louder, but I found them fat and unpleasant. The air flowing through my surroundings wanted to choke me down.

I was met with silence. Not the kind of silence that came after an argument or before a punishment, but a heavier kind, a suffocating emptiness that hung in the air.

There were no angry footsteps to run from. The absence of it all was almost worse. I had been so used to the voices, the tension, the feeling of never being enough that the silence felt like a different kind of punishment.

It echoed in the walls as if the house itself was swallowing me whole.

Time stretched into a kind of stillness that wasn't peaceful; it felt hollow.

I looked around at the dust settling on the countertops, at the small, leftover things my family had forgotten to take, a thing that hadn't left me in this nightmare.

There was no life left here, no warmth, just the remnants of a house that no longer felt like home.

It was as if I had been left in the shell of something that used to be filled. Filled with anger and unpleasant voices and expressions leading to punishments justifying and proving how imperfect and silly I am, now abandoned to figure out its emptiness alone.

How dare you?! How dare you leave me like that, I want you guys back! Said a voice in my head, to which I responded with utter silence and ignorance.

They were abusive anyway. Aren't you tired of all of those shoutings and living in constant fear of never knowing when they'll be pointing a mistake of yours out of nowhere and rewarding you with a handful of shouting and yelling, said the other voice.

For me, even dust didn't turn into gold. I responded with the same silence the last time I did but with a spark because a glimpse of a swing landed in my eyes. The swing that we had on the veranda. I ran toward it and held it. But... *something was odd.*

I wasn't starving anymore. The thought struck me! *Not starving,* but also not... anything. Not yearning, not waiting. Not even hoping for a change that wouldn't come. And for a moment, that realisation felt heavier than hunger itself.

It was strange, sitting there with the sudden sense that I needed nothing from this place anymore, almost as if every thread binding me to this house had snapped in the quiet.

I ran my fingers over the cold rope of the swing. Maybe this is what freedom feels like, I thought, or maybe this is just another kind of starvation.

The emptiness of the house surrounded me like a fog, thick and suffocating, and I was left to grapple with its weight. The walls, once echoing with the screams that ripped through my sanity, now felt like a tomb, a mausoleum for the memories that haunted me.

I closed my eyes, trying to shake off the remnants of the past, but every time I thought I had escaped, another shadow crept in. I was abandoned not just by them but by the childhood I was supposed to have. I could almost hear the mocking laughter of those who thrived in homes filled with love, their joy a distant melody that played just beyond my reach. I felt like a ghost lingering in the space where life used to exist but now only saw death's quiet grip.

The swing creaked softly, a hollow sound that reverberated through the air, mocking me in its simplicity. It reminded me of moments when I was pushed on it, carefree, yet in the back of my mind was always the knowledge that each laugh had a price, one I was still paying. Here, in this ghost of a home, even the echoes of happiness felt tainted.

I stood up abruptly, anger igniting a fire within me. How dare they leave me with this emptiness? How dare they pretend their absence was a gift? The silence screamed in response, mocking my outrage, reminding me that they were the ones who made me feel worthless, who fed me the poison of neglect under the guise of care.

As I paced the room, my thoughts spiralled deeper into darkness. I could see their faces, twisted in anger, the words laced with venom, and the punishments that turned my skin into a canvas of scars. I wanted to tear down the memories that clung to me like shadows, but they were ingrained in my very being.

In this shell of a house, I was left to sift through the debris of my existence, love replaced with abuse, laughter silenced by fear.

Suddenly, the hunger for their presence twisted into a hunger for something more, a desire to reclaim my voice, to break free from the chains of their expectations, and to find a way to fill the void they had left behind.

But how?

I thought, a bitter smile creeping across my face. How does one escape the prison built by their own blood? But is this a prison?!

Asked a voice in my head. To which my silence drowned me into utter shamefulness about myself. And as usual, I again ignored the voices in my head along with a million possibilities and the elegance of freedom in my head.

I snapped out of all of that and walked towards the kitchen. Entered the kitchen and grabbed a pan and the box of coffee. I learned to make it a few days ago, then, and decided to make myself a cup of coffee because I thought that would be relaxing and relieving, to be honest.

I turned on the electric stove, the hum of the coils heating up, cutting through the silence, sharp and cold. The kitchen felt hollow, both endless and suffocating.

As the water in the pot started to heat, I watched tiny bubbles gather at the bottom, held down by the weight of the past, then break free one by one, clawing their way to the surface.

It was like all those bitter thoughts I'd buried were struggling up, uninvited, reminding me that they hadn't found peace, either. Just like me.

I grabbed the coffee, my hands shaking slightly. I'd only learned to make it a few days ago. A simple thing, really! Boil, stir, pour! But it felt like a lifeline. I needed to control something, anything, in this world that kept pulling me under.

The coffee hit my tongue, a punch of bitterness that twisted my face, but I forced myself to take it in, letting it sear my throat. It was better than the silence. Better than the feeling of drowning in the empty house.

But the quiet didn't break. The kitchen stayed still, indifferent. I felt like I'd been abandoned here, left to fend off ghosts with nothing but a bitter cup in my hand.

The coffee had long gone cold, just like the remnants of warmth that used to fill these walls, now replaced with an oppressive silence that weighed down on me.

I took a sip, the taste harsh and stale, reminding me that comfort was a distant memory, one I'd never be able to reclaim.

I let the cup slip through my fingers, clattering to the floor, shattering like the remnants of my sanity. It felt fitting a representation of the fragile existence I'd been trying to piece together in this fractured space.

I stood in the middle of the kitchen, engulfed by the memories that swirled around me like an unwelcome fog. Each corner whispered secrets of the past, each object a reminder of the chaos that lingered just beneath the surface.

The fridge hummed softly, a mocking lullaby in the silence, as I drifted back to the times when laughter filled this space. I could almost hear it now–the echo of my mother's laughter mingling with the clinking of dishes, a sound that had once felt like home but now resonated with a haunting emptiness. The memory of her smile was a knife to my heart, sharp and unyielding.

Why did she have to be so perfect? So bright against the backdrop of my dark existence? I gritted my teeth, anger bubbling just beneath the surface, mingling with the familiar taste of betrayal. I had spent countless nights replaying those moments, dissecting them like a morbid puzzle.

I thought about how her laughter had faded into the background, overshadowed by the storms of rage that brewed in our home, a silent spectator to the chaos.

The laughter I yearned for had been nothing but a mirage, a fleeting glimpse of what could have been if only our lives had unfolded differently.

But it was gone now, lost in the shadows that clung to every surface, suffocating me in their grasp. I felt like a ghost haunting my own memories, unable to move on, trapped in a cycle of regret and longing.

The emptiness was palpable, a constant reminder of the love I had sought but never truly felt.

As I stood there, the world outside came alive with sounds I had long tried to ignore: the laughter of children playing and the distant hum of conversations that drifted in through the open window.

It felt foreign, alien. Their joy was a stark contrast to the desolation that had become my reality. I wanted to shut it out, to retreat further into my cocoon of darkness, but I was stuck in this limbo, caught between the freedom I craved and the chains of my own making.

Then, without warning, the familiar sound of a car engine pierced through the silence, slicing through the haze of memories like a knife. My heart dropped, each beat echoing the dread pooling in my stomach.

The engine was followed by the unmistakable sound of a car door slamming shut, reverberating against the walls of my mind. I felt my breath hitch in my throat as the reality of their presence began to settle over me like a thick fog.

They were here.

My parents.

My father! He came back from rehab like a shadow when returning to my life, bringing himself and the weight of unkept promises with him. When I last saw him, he was that shell of a man lost in the haze of addiction.

Yet, something within me stirred that primal fear when he was coming home. It was as if every second of each lonely moment apart was one more to the final ticking before all this dread materialised in a confrontation, marching like a slow march of doom into the darkness threatening us for as long as we had lived.

My feet remained rooted on the kitchen ground, but everything outside took shape in a haze. Panic was melting my insides like fire as I sped through a million arguments, all those hurtful words that had careened off of these walls and left scars that could never be healed.

With every beat of my heart, there was a reminder of what lay in wait between us, of the conflict ahead: How would I face him after this long? After everything that had passed between us?

And then I heard them. A muffled murmur of familiar voices coming from the driveway vibrated through the air with an almost otherworldly tension.

My mother's high-pitched laughter, once a warm sound, was now ice on my very skin. My father's voice was lower, an authoritative timbre that used to choke my heart with fear, reminding me of the monster lurking just beneath.

Laughter sounded within the hollowness, and my guts rolled over. That was one sweet sound, a thing that could always be assumed as a reason for merriment, but now that it had replaced the knell tolling for the return of the tormentor, I stepped back into the shadows, wanting to, again and again, fade out as a thief in the night. It was too late, though. They were here, entrapping me into their reality once again.

Seeing my father's face had caused chills down my spine, a reminder of the tempest he had brought along. Would he be sober today? Would he slip back into old patterns, back into the cycle of rage and disappointment?

Questions flooded my mind: questions about the chaos, the nights in my room, and the shouting that rattled the very foundations of our home. A warped sense of fear crept in as I tried to catch the emotions flowing within the resentment, the fear, and the yearning for something I could never achieve.

"Maybe this is what freedom feels like," I thought to myself, but even in my head, the thought had a lie written all over it. This was not freedom-it was a new kind of captivity.

The darkness inside of me stirred again; it reminded me that those demons of my past were never far behind, lurking in the shadows, waiting for the right moment to drag me back into their suffocating embrace.

The kitchen felt stuffy and silent - a cruel reminder of what lay ahead. I could almost hear the muffled but distinct echo of my father's voice, the spectre of the man who came back from rehab to disrupt whatever fragile peace that I had managed to carve out for myself. Would he walk in and ruin this hollow moment of solitude, turning it into a battlefield once again?

The rumble of the engine outside grew louder in my ears, signalling their arrival. But a part of me wanted to run away and hide in some hole somewhere from the reality of their coming, for I was held in that same cycle of fear that had consumed most of my childhood.

Their angry shouts and hard words are poison to my memory, and every corner of that house seems infected. I hate the fact that they were there, a flickering candle in a storm, where a gust of wind could blow it out.

The quietness of the kitchen weighed heavy on those shoulders, antithetical to the turmoil there. I could almost hear the anger of years ago, the echoes of yells and accusations still tormenting me.

These memories wrapped around me like a second skin, reminding me of the worst person I had been in their eyes every minute shared with my family, always poised on the threshold of accepting and rejecting me, always on the watch for the next storm that would rip away the fragile façade of normalcy.

It was so pleasing to be in my room: darkness covered me like a blanket of soft comfort that would conceal me from the world outside. Alone, I could escape the unbearable weight of their expectations, the stinging words that pierced my soul.

The shadows in my sanctuary felt so companionable rather than menacing because they knew the depth of my suffering, a knowing my family could never share. Out there in the world of people, I was no more than this hunk of broken glass, but in my isolation, I could be whatever or nothing, judge-free.

I stood there with coffee in hand, but the lurking tendrils of despair gripped tight around me. How does one move on from a past that feels like the shadow of a ghost? I was my own prisoner, handcuffed with memories that would never allow me to forget.

It was easier to hide under blankets of dark rather than face the organised chaos that muddled in the familial storm. In my room, peace reigned--a complete silence counter to the emotional noise pulsating through the house.

The far-off rumble of an engine was stammering back into my thoughts, a familiar rumble that made my shivers run. They were coming back with them would come the oppressive atmosphere I hated to be surrounded by.

I was expecting yet another wave that would probably overwhelm me with all the fear, anger, and deep angst of abandonment that presented itself whenever they were near.

In that silence, with walls still punctuated by all the sounds I've heard growing up, I still wonder what it would be like to step out of this cage I was raised in. But stepping out? Could that possibly be an option? Facing the world outside seemed heavy enough to weigh on my shoulders, like staying locked inside.

I didn't know how to play out there, how to fit in, or even if I wanted to. Each memory, each scar, seemed to remind me that I didn't belong in either world, one inside or the one outside.

The presence of them all around me now churned my stomach, an action that came naturally to me now, almost like a reflex I couldn't turn off. It was safer carrying this weight alone than it was to be with others.

And then there was, in the back of my mind, a sense that whatever was happening here, whatever was shaping me, marked me too deep for anyone to see or understand.

CHAPTER THREE

Shaking Feet

The thought of company made my stomach twist. This is a reaction now, a reflex I couldn't seem to get rid of. It was as if solitude meant safer and simpler, even when it meant carrying all that burden around alone. And somehow, in the back of my mind, I knew whatever was happening here, whatever was shaping me, had left a mark too deep for others to see or understand.

In those quiet moments, I started to wonder if the walls I built to keep

others out were really prisons I'd made for myself.

There is a heaviness that sits in the pit of your stomach when you walk into a room and feel like everyone is looking at you, even though nobody is.

It can't be explained, but it's there. Pressure in your chest, sweat bursting out on your palms, the feeling that you are too much and not enough at the same time. Social anxiety isn't shyness. It's the noise of all the things people don't say, their judgments, their whispers. The weight of every word and every silence crushes you.

Like I have been walking through life with a target on my back, one placed there the day I was born, carved into me by people who were supposed to care: my family, silent expectations, constant criticisms, voices haunting me.

Not the yelling, but the looks. The silences. The way I always got things wrong, no matter what I did. They'd break me down with their words and pretend that nothing ever transpired.

And somehow, that shit doesn't leave you when you leave. It's in your bones. Every other social contact is essentially a performance, and I walk on a tightrope, hoping not to fall but knowing that I will every time.

There's always that voice in my head, waiting for me to slip, waiting for me to say the wrong thing, waiting for me to be me and get it wrong.

And when do I slip? When do I open my mouth too wide or say too much? That's when it strikes and knocks the life out of me. So I keep quiet, become tiny and hide behind the faces in the crowd, for then the voices aren't so loud.

I'd rather be lonely in my room than out there, exposed and vulnerable. In my room, at least, no one will judge me. In my room, at least, I could pretend that the world hadn't taught me how worthless I was.

And I am not alone in this; many of you guys would be able to relate to this thing, too. This crowd feels awkward while walking around with your heads down and hiding behind the loud songs playing in your headphones in public places.

But it doesn't stop there, does it? Social anxiety isn't the fear of being seen-it's the fear of being noticed. Every step outside is walking on a stage with eyes pricking through the skin, judging, mocking, and dissecting.

The air around your own body feels more substantial like it is pressing down upon your chest and squeezing out anything you might have had the temerity to say.

And the worst part? No one even looks at you, and then gazes out the window at the storm inside. You avoid eye contact, clutch your bag harder, expecting a blow, and maybe stumble over your phone in your pocket. To them, you are quiet. To you, you're drowning.

And for all of us carrying scars from this childhood, this anxiety is not just a state of mind but rather a way of survival. Every stuttering step, every misstep may represent that trigger, the abhorrent flashback reminding us of voices that once berated us for not being good enough.

The pressure to never make a mistake, to never blow it, lives in every little transaction-from ordering food to answering the phone and even just sitting in a room with people you don't know.

We'd rather remain invisible and let the world go by than possibly incur another wound. And yet, day after day, we fight this apparently invisible war, hoping no one will notice how hard we're trying to be.

It feels like the walls of your very own mind are closing in. Thoughts spin on and surround you without anything to handle them. Did I walk funny?

Do they think my hands shake? Was my laughter too loud? The questions seem endless as they keep digging into a never-ending well of self-doubt.

And no matter how much you rationalise, the voice in your head refuses to quiet down, it whispers, screams, mocks. It doesn't matter how many times you've been told, "Nobody's watching you." Because for you, everybody is.

And then there's the avoidance. The parties you skip, the invitations you decline, the friendships you let fizzle out because the thought of being seen, really seen, is too unbearable.

People call it being introverted, shy, or reserved. Not that it is in any way a matter of choice. It's a means of protection from that overwhelming fear of perhaps saying something stupid, perhaps being laughed at, perhaps judged.

It's about avoiding the shame you have been carrying around for as long as you can remember. And as much as you need connection, the risk is too high, so you stay within your airtight little bubble, even when it suffocates.

It's funny how loneliness doesn't just make you isolationist; it becomes hunger. A hunger for connection, validation, anything to drown out the silence of your own thoughts.

And then, hunger can become unbearable, and you stretch out, not with discernment, but with desperation. You do not examine what is offered; you only see that someone offers something. And that is how it happens, isn't it? How people like us, those with shaking feet and shaking voices, fall into the wrong circles.

They aren't good people. You know that. But they're there. And when they laugh, you tell yourself it's with you and not at you. When they give any attention to you, you convince yourself that it is because you matter, not that they need someone to pass around when the mood strikes.

They give you scraps of belonging, and you devour them like a starving dog. Because what's the alternative? Being alone? No, that's worse. That's unbearable.

And slowly but surely, they shape you. You grow quieter, shrinking deeper into the shadows of their loud, brash voices, acting like words don't sting.

Or you become them, trying on a mask of cruelty that doesn't fit right and hoping it will make you just as bad as they are. It never will. Deep down, you know you're just their punch line. But at least you exist in a place, don't you? At least now, at this point, you see yourself, and you do not stand there in horror alone.

But the worst part of all is- you don't even feel resentful towards them. How could you when you so willingly handed over your soul to them?

You were one such desperate soul trying to run from the emptiness that you practically walked into another kind of hell. Sometimes, you wonder if they knew just how breakable you were.

Whether they spotted cracks in your armour and chose to exploit them or whether they simply sized you up like they size up everyone. Doesn't matter. You are bruised by them but also by the realisation that you allowed it.

And now, still no pity. No anguished monologue of how everything was so terribly wrong. It wasn't wrong-it was predictable. People like us, scarred, unsure, and aching for acceptance, are easy prey.

But here's the thing: we're not just prey, are we? We survive. We adapt. And somewhere in that mess of bad choices and worse friendships, we learn to see the world for what it is: Not fair. Not kind. But it's something we can navigate, even if it's on shaking feet.

But navigating doesn't mean thriving. It doesn't mean belonging. It means getting by. It means finding corners to hide in when the world feels too big and too loud. It means biting your tongue when the wrong words spill out, choking on apologies you're too tired to offer.

It means to adapt, not fit in, but not to stand out, to be part of the background noise of everyone's lives. Survival is far from glamorous; it is desperate, raw, and ugly.

And as much as I want to say that I have mastered it, I haven't. I learned just the patterns, the unspoken rules: smile when you're supposed to, nod when you're expected to, laugh when the joke's on you, particularly if it's on you.

Because nothing keeps people off guard better than self-deprecation, it's the easiest reminder they don't have anything to worry about, just another face in the crowd, harmless and forgettable.

But here's the thing: even the act of blending in leaves its own scars. It takes pieces of you-small ones at first, so insignificant you barely notice.

A laugh you don't mean, a word you don't say, a thought you bury because it's easier that way. And then, one day, you look in the mirror and realise you've whittled yourself down to nothing. A shell of the person you might have been if only you'd been allowed to exist as yourself.

Except I was never quite sure which "self" that was. The afraid child who sat at the edges of the playground, refusing to step forward? The teenager nodded along to the joke they didn't understand. Or the adult now sitting in silence, watching how the shadows creep across the wall, asking aloud how it came to be so quiet.

The thing is, I miss nothing I never had: not love or understanding or a sense of home. Those are just losses, concepts that never really made sense: colours you can't define or sounds you've never heard.

You can't grieve what you didn't know existed. You can still, however, feel the ache of something that was never there, such as phantom limbs that nobody ever had to begin with.

The cruellest part of this is not that somewhere deep down, I know that it's all there can be. This fractured version of existence.

A half-life of pretending, of adjusting, of surviving. And maybe this will ever be the case. And then, as if my body wanted to remind me just how much it carried, there was pain in my neck.

A dull, persistent ache that crept in with every downward glance, every hunched shoulder. It's strange how something so small, a tilt of the head, can shape you. Not just your posture but your entire being.

People love to point it out. "Tech neck," they call it, laugh like they have cracked some sort of code. "Too much time on your phone, huh?"

As if my slumped posture were a joke. They see a neck that curves after hours spent scrolling and bingeing and wasting away in front of a screen. They don't see the years that bent me.

It wasn't screened. It wasn't the glow of a phone or the hum of a laptop. It was the floor. The pavement. The cracks between tiles. The only safe place to look when eyes feel like weapons and even shadows carry threats.

The weight of everything that comes before words and actions and silences pushes my chin down, forcing me into this constant bow of avoidance.

In crowds, I stuck my eyes on my feet. In school, it was on my desk. Back home, the eyes moved to the spaces in people: their hands, their laps, anything but their faces. A habit now. The instinct was a burden now. And the burden was me. A hunched figure. A stiff neck. A monument to everything I never said.

Years of looking down left their mark. Now, even when there's no one around, no eyes to dodge, my neck stays bent, like it's forgotten how to stand tall. It's not rebellion against technology or some ironic symbol of modern times; it's survival etched into my spine.

And the funniest part? They point out that it's my fault like I have control over it. Like I ever sat down one day and decided to be a form of every unspoken word, every swallowed scream, every missed glance. This is not tech neck. It is a trauma neck. A legacy of fear carved bone deep.

But the weight of it isn't just mine, is it? The heads bent low in the crowd, the awkward hunch as we shrunk ourselves smaller, quieter. We look down because looking up feels like too much. Too bold. Too vulnerable. Too exposed. And that's the thing about weight-it's heavy, but it's shared.

The ground never swallowed me, no matter how hard I stared. It stayed firm, unyielding, reminding me of my need to be stuck. And here I stand. Bent over, twisted under, hunched over but standing. And that might be all that matters for now.

Does it make sense? Do we make sense? Or do we carry necks full of stories we'll never tell?

I could've spun this into something brighter, something hopeful. But that wouldn't be honest, would it? I am not here to inspire you; I am here to remind you that you are not alone in this mess. That your hunched neck, your downward glance, isn't just a flaw–it's a survival skill.

So look down if you must. Bend your head, and let the weight press against your shoulders. But don't mistake it for weakness. Someday, you'll look up not because the world has changed but because you've carried the weight long enough to know you can.

CHAPTER FOUR

Early Mornings

They say school shapes a child, but for some of us, it merely adds another layer of silence to the ones we already carry. The kind of silence that isn't peaceful–it's heavy, oppressive, always on the verge of cracking.

For me, mornings weren't chaotic like you'd imagine in a typical desi household. There were no rushed goodbyes, no playful scoldings about forgotten homework. Just the suffocating stillness that settled in every corner of my house.

I'd wake up, get ready, and step into my uniform with robotic precision, avoiding eye contact even with my own reflection. The air at home always felt like it could shatter with the wrong move, the wrong word, the wrong thought.

School is another different kind of quiet but not so much the kind. I wouldn't say it was the kind of place that showed warmth or gave safety. It was just another space where I learned how to keep my head down- literally and metaphorically.

Nobody warns you that getting older is largely a process of simply learning how to exist in spaces that seem to not care if you're there at all.

Or how by the time you consciously realise that you've already begun to feel like a ghost in the room. In school, I wasn't that bullied kid-not in the obvious, loud way, but I wasn't an "in" kid, either. I was the one nobody bothered to notice. And that kind of loneliness isn't any different.

I'd sit there, unseen among the faces, watching the world go by around me like a play I was never meant to play. But what's worse? Being ignored or being stared at like a specimen? The looks weren't of interest.

No, they were of curiosity, of pity. They saw something different, something broken. And they stayed the hell away from it - the silence, the heaviness with every step.

But here's the thing about being ignored: You come to believe it. That you don't matter, that you're not worth paying attention to, it isn't just the world that stops seeing you—it's you, too. You learn to believe your absence.

I didn't need their approval, though. I knew what they thought. The teachers? They had their way of showing their indifference. Some were quiet about it, some were open about it, but none of them ever bothered to check beneath the surface.

I wasn't the problem, they were. But I had learned long ago that problems don't get solved, they just get ignored until they disappear.

I would sit there with my back all hunched over, staring at the blank page in front of me, my eyes scanning the words as they all blended into some sort of letter soup I could not connect.

I didn't even bother trying. Why bother pretending to be part of something? The whole damn room felt like a cage, but those bars weren't there, caging me in. They were invisible, expectations and judgments that slid across my skin like poison.

And then the teachers. Some of them had the kind that made me feel like they could see right through me, but not in the way I wanted.

They didn't see a person. They saw a failure, a future failure. A name on a piece of paper they could barely recall, a body they had to fill for a chair. Some were violent in their words, a glance sharp enough to cut yet not sharp enough to bleed. Others were subtler–quiet in cruelty, the kind that made you feel small without ever uttering a single word.

But what was it to me? Not much, really. I mean, by the time I walked into those classrooms, I had already accepted that I wasn't cut out for this world. My body was a thing I carried around, a ghost that walked without purpose.

I did not belong in the noisiness of the world, and I certainly did not belong in the loud, ignorant chatter of my classmates. They talked, and I listened, but I didn't understand. It seemed that they were a different species, foreign to me.

There were moments, though, where the silence felt louder than anything else. Like when the teacher's voice would cut through the hum of my thoughts, and I'd realise everyone else was listening, but I wasn't. And I'd feel it—the weight of not belonging not just to the class but to the world itself.

I didn't like them. I didn't fit the script. I was the kid who looked away when everybody else was laughing. I didn't make the jokes, and I didn't join in their games. I was the one they forgot when the bell rang. And I hated it.

I hated how they all moved so effortlessly, how they belonged to spaces that I couldn't even breathe in. But most of all, I hated myself for wanting to be a part of them, for wanting to fit in with a crowd that didn't give a shit about me.

The classroom was always like a battlefield as if I were a soldier who had long since given up on the war. The other kids had it easy; they ran through the day as if it were second nature, exchanging words, passing notes, and laughing as if they weren't carrying their own burdens.

I don't know how. I didn't know how to be like them. Every morning, I sat there like a stone, my body stiff, my mind running through that same repeating cycle of thoughts —Don't look at anyone. Don't say anything. Keep your head down.

Those teachers always watched me. Their eyes were full of questions their mouths never asked. "Why don't you participate? " they'd ask, as if they hadn't listened closely. As if I could just open my mouth, and words would spill out of it, like everyone else. But I couldn't. I never could. I wasn't built for this, not with all the shit in my head.

I'd sit there in silence, heart pounding in my chest, praying that nobody noticed how tightly I was wound, how much I was trying not to crack under the pressure of it all. They thought I was shy. One of those kids who would just grow out of it. It was never about being shy. It was about survival.

It was about keeping the walls up because if I didn't, everything would come crashing down on me. The silence at home was not just quiet. It was suffocating. It was a presence that sat heavy in every corner, every room.

It pressed on my chest and kept my throat closed. I never learned to speak, to express myself in a way that meant something. There was nothing to say at home. No one to listen.

It wasn't teachers who made me feel so small—it was the fucking environment I came from. They didn't know what it was like to live in a house where no one talked, no one cared to understand.

Where my father was nowhere to be found, lost in his destructive ordeals, and my mother so caught up in her grief that I was nothing more than a spectre barely visible in the background. She had no wherewithal to notice, let alone find any energy to teach me how to move through the world.

I learned how to hide, how to disappear, how to keep my head down and not draw attention.

I didn't even know how to be a person in a room full of people. So, yeah, I resented the teachers. Their voices, their demands, their expectations. I hated how they pushed me, how they tried to make me be something I wasn't ready to be. But they weren't the problem.

I was.

I walked into that classroom each day as someone broke, already moulded by the silence and darkness that had become my home.

I didn't mumble; I was afraid. I was afraid they would see me and notice me because if they saw me, they'd see everything I was running from.

They'd see the cracks in my soul, the way my body was a shell that I didn't even know how to live in. The teachers, they weren't the ones who broke me.

They were just doing their fucking job, asking questions, giving assignments, trying to make me fit in to be a part of something.

But I couldn't. I couldn't be a part of anything because I wasn't whole. My problem was that I wasn't sure if I was real. I was just trying to find my way through the day without anyone noticing that my mind was a constant battlefield.

I was already losing the fight before it even started.

Yet they didn't get it. They couldn't. How could they? They were not seeing the world in the same way I was. To them, this was just a classroom.

To me, it was a prison. It was a place where I went to put on a face, pretend to be something I wasn't, just to make it through the day without completely losing myself in the process.

But the truth?

The thing is, it wasn't their fault. It was mine. I built this cage, this wall around myself, and every day I went to school, I was carrying it there. Every word that was expected of me, every smile, every try at normalcy was another brick I had to lay down in the prison I'd made. But no teacher, no matter how benevolent, could break it down. Only I could do that. But I didn't know how.

It was not unusual for me to cry in class, with tears streaming down my cheeks uncontrollably, for no apparent reason. Other kids didn't harass those are cases that make all the headlines. I wasn't even some kind of outcast, so there couldn't be any obvious "cause".

But then, I couldn't have articulated the reason. It wasn't a stomachache, something I could excuse with a simple "headache" or "not feeling well."

No, this was something else, something darker, something that started long before I ever sat in that classroom. It was the weight of the place I came from–the home I was supposed to find refuge in but only found torment instead.

In the middle of a lesson, I would clutch my stomach in pain while hiding behind a pasty smile. But to outsiders, nothing was showing; the pain was always inside me, though it wasn't just physical; everything was being eaten away from the inside out.

For that weight, my little body couldn't carry the pressure it had taken, living in that house, nobody said a word, the heavy silence screamed louder than any fight could.

I thought it was just a stomach ache, something bad to have eaten; not food-it was the weight of the goddamn world. It was my mind, an already breaking ten-year-old mind, cracking and breaking under the weight of everything that was happening at home.

The gut-wrenching, nauseous feeling was not a passing sickness. It was anxiety. It was my soul breaking down somewhere where I couldn't scream or cry, so my body did it for me.

I mean, the truth is, I didn't know what it was then. I just thought I was weak, thought I was fucking fragile. I didn't know that the environment that I grew up in, this violent silence that fills that space every day, was killing me.

No one told me. It was done to me piecemeal without me even knowing. I just assumed that's the way it was. That's the problem with growing up in it. You don't realise how abnormal it is until you are out of it.

I didn't know my stomach was so twisted because my heart had been broken a thousand times without me even noticing.

When I look back now, I realise I wasn't just some kid who had some random stomach ache. I was carrying anxiety around like some fucking anchor, dragging it with me to school every day. It was that nagging feeling as if something was about to blow inside me, and I could not do anything about it.

I couldn't breathe, couldn't think properly, couldn't speak without the whole world caving in around me. I'd sit there, frozen in place, eyes glued to the desk, pretending it wasn't happening. But it was. And I couldn't stop it.

I was ten years old, a kid, drowning. My body was so small as if it had to hold everything. That is, everything it wasn't equipped for.

But the worst part? I had no idea how to make it stop. I thought that if I just remained quiet enough, that if I just continued pretending everything was fine, the pain would go away. It didn't. Never did. It only got worse.

And yet, I can look back now and see it for what it was. I wasn't just sick; I wasn't just weak. I was fucking drowning in the aftermath of a home that I didn't know how to love, a house where silence is louder than any scream. Anxiety isn't a stomach ache. It was a daily, oppressive thing that made every day like a fight I would forever lose.

It was only years later that I finally understood pain was something I couldn't escape. It wasn't something that was going to disappear. It was a part of me, a part that I had to learn to live with, even when I didn't understand it.

It wasn't the teachers. It wasn't the kids. It wasn't even the school that carved the jagged edges of my anxiety into my being. It was them.

My family–the architects of my fragility. The ones who should have been my refuge, my foundation, but instead became the silent architects of my undoing.

My anxiety wasn't born out of nowhere; it was built, brick by brick, in the suffocating walls of that house. Every slam of a door, every sharp inhale before an argument, every forced smile at a dinner table that reeked of unspoken resentment–it all seeped into me like a slow poison.

Do you know what silence feels like when it's not peaceful? It's a monster that grows in the quiet. It's the breath you hold, the words you swallow, the tension pressed so tight against your chest that you forget what air should feel like.

My house wasn't loud at all hours of the day. The chaos didn't happen forever. There were times when silence was worse. It had the sort of quiet that set your stomach plummeting as your ears strained, desperate for something to shatter.

And it did break. Not necessarily in the ways people might imagine. Not in the shouting matches or broken plates, though those happened plenty of times.

It broke within the cracks that formed inside of me, the way I froze at the sound of raised voices, the way I learned to fade into corners and take up as little space as possible because space in that house was dangerous.

Attention was dangerous. And just because you were invisible wouldn't save you, but at least it diminished the blows – the verbal ones, the emotional ones, the ones without marks to show but aching scars you could never remember.

It's not a mystery why I became the way I am. My voice caught in my throat, not because I was shy but because speaking up felt like tempting fate. My hands shook in public, not because I was nervous but because I had been taught to fear being noticed.

My shoulders hunched, my neck bent–not because of screens but because looking up always felt like an invitation for more pain.

They rewired me. My body became the map of their chaos. My stomach didn't twist out of nowhere; it twisted because I was raised to digest their tension, their unresolved issues, and their suffocating expectations. The pit in my stomach that gnawed at me, that I once thought was illness or weakness, wasn't that at all.

It was anxiety–the kind that takes root so deep you forget it's there until it grips you without warning. I used to cry in class, a quiet, restrained kind of crying that drew no attention because that's what I'd been taught: never draw attention.

Teachers thought it was a stomachache, and I didn't correct them because, in a way, it was. It was a sickness born in my gut, fed by years of turmoil that a 10-year-old had no way to name, no way to understand.

Still, during all this, they never saw it. The wreckage my family carried out just kept moving. The sensitive, the dramatic or little too reserved ones are what my family painted me.

Never did they take some time to wonder why. Connecting those dots of their wars to the one left and raged within me had not been considered at that point.

They raised me but mostly shaped me, for the good or ill–mostly to their disadvantage. They delivered this anxiety to me by an inheritance, wrapped around themselves with unresolved trauma and dysfunction.

And they left the solving up to me to uncurl all the knots and bear the weight they hadn't carried. And as it sits here, those years down, with the aching, the tension and unrest, I cannot even ask if they'd known, whether they even care.

Here's the thing, though: I care. I have to. Because I am the one left holding the pieces of their chaos, trying to build something out of the ruins they left behind.

CHAPTER FIVE

Eyes On Me

It's funny how people think self-esteem is about confidence. It is something you can slap on with a better outfit or a compliment from someone who barely knows you. People say things like, "Believe in yourself," as if that has ever been enough to drown out the voices in your head. The thing is, self-esteem doesn't build itself in a vacuum. It's shaped, beaten, and bruised by the hands that were supposed to hold you steady.

And if those hands weaken–if they grip too hard or release too soon–the marks linger, never completely healing. You go about your life with those unseeable fingerprints on you, like a crime scene that was never dusted or cleaned up.

You begin to misunderstand their indifference as your flaw, their silence as your fault. It is something heavy to carry around when no one else seems to care about the weight of it.

Not me, though, right? We all had those moments where we sat in a room with people around us but felt like we didn't belong. Seeing someone's lips move and hearing something entirely different.

You're not enough. You're never enough.

It is not their words; it is yours. It is the background track playing nonstop at every turn of everything you do, every decision you make. And the worst part? You don't even realise it started long before you knew what self-esteem even meant.

Perhaps it was in the way your parents dismissed you, not with words but with looks. The kind of looks that say, "Why aren't you better? " without ever having to spell it out. Perhaps it was in those minute details in school when someone laughed a little too long, or the teacher called on another person when your hand was raised way above all others. Those are not just memories–they're blueprints.

They build the blueprints of your insecurities, brick by brick so that you live in a house you never constructed but cannot seem to find an exit from.

For me, it wasn't one of those moments. It was the air at home thick with expectations that I couldn't quite meet and punishments that seemed fitting for crimes I had never committed. It was the silence at the dinner table, where words felt like landmines, and I was the only one stepping on them. And when I stepped into the world outside, I thought it would be different. I thought maybe I could breathe out there.

But the echoes followed me, stitched into the fabric of who I was.

Tell me, do you ever wonder where it all went wrong? Was it a single moment or a thousand tiny cuts that bled you dry? And how many of us are out there, standing in mirrors, dissecting ourselves like lab experiments, trying to find what's so fundamentally broken? It's not just about self-esteem. It's about survival.

Let's be honest—it never has been about confidence, has it? It's about trying to feel human in a world that seems to remind you that you are never enough constantly. It's about dragging yourself through the day on the weight of what they said, what they didn't say, what you said to yourself when nobody else was in the room.

It's about looking into the mirror and wishing that it might reflect something you could call your own, something you could love. That's where my story bleeds into yours, doesn't it?

Because this isn't just about me. *It's about us*, the ones who carry those invisible scars and wonder if anyone else sees them. The ones who fight battles no one claps for and survive nights no one remembers. But that's the thing we survive. Even when it feels like we shouldn't, even when the world tells us we can't. We're still here. And maybe that's something, even if it doesn't feel like much.

The mirror didn't lie, but it didn't need to. Its job was simpler: to reflect back on the version of me I hated the most, the one I'd been running from my entire life. It didn't show me a person–it showed a shell, a hollowed-out version of what could have been. Every glance was a reminder, sharp and merciless: You're not enough. You never were.

The cracks weren't in the glass. They were in me, carved deep and jagged, left behind by years of carefully measured silences, cutting words masquerading as advice, and the suffocating weight of expectations I couldn't meet. Whenever someone said, *"You'd be better if...,"* it wasn't a suggestion–it was a verdict. If I was better, maybe they would've loved me. If I was better, maybe I would've loved myself.

But they didn't give me love or acceptance; they gave me scraps. And you don't build self-esteem with scraps. You build doubt. You build a fragile version of yourself that falls apart the moment someone looks too closely. They didn't need to tell me I wasn't good enough; I'd already mastered the art of tearing myself apart before anyone else could.

It wasn't just the mirror, though. It was the looks, the careful pauses, the comparisons they pretended weren't cruel. It was the way the house echoed with conditional love, love that came with rules, with thresholds I never seemed to meet. And even when I did, it felt temporary, fleeting, like it could be snatched away the moment I slipped.

People talk about self-esteem like it's a skill you learn like it's some DIY project where you patch yourself up and walk away fixed. They don't tell you the truth: that self-esteem isn't built in isolation. It's handed down. It's taught. And when you grow up with none, you don't start from scratch–you start in debt.

No one will ever explain how impossible it feels to love oneself when spending a lifetime being taught the fact that nobody loves one. *"Be kind to yourself,"* as if kindness had any hope to grow with such poisoned soil after neglectful years of time, it seems. The reality? Kindness doesn't grow there. Only survival. Only the possibility of existing with a heart wanting not to exist.

The mirror isn't cruel, it's just indifferent, reflecting the truth you were so desperate to run from, the fact that the world doesn't give a damn, and neither did you. It reveals your burden, the guilt someone else never should have assigned you, but somehow you carried nonetheless.

And every time you look, you almost expect something different, better than this. But there, staring back at you is all this mess they left, which dares you to clean up what they broke.

And that is the cruellest thing of all: it's not even your fault that the person you are the person you most despise- their negligence, their lack of caring, their incapability of giving you any kind of tools to form yourself, no one can see this.

No one wants to see this because it is far easier to tell you to blame yourself and tell you you are weak every bruise and every break is something you opted for.

You didn't choose this. You didn't choose to wake up every day hating the face in the mirror, questioning why you even bother to exist. But now, you carry it alone–the mess they made, the weight they left you with. And somehow, they expect you to smile through it, to thank them for the lessons, to pretend it didn't break you in ways you'll never fully recover from.

But the truth of the matter is you don't recover. You simply learn to exist with the mess, the cracks, the weight. You learn to survive, and survival's got more in line with the definition of the word for punishment rather than progress. You look at the mirror, not at you but at the reflection of each reason that brought you this way. Maybe one day you stop gazing into the glass at all.

Do you ever feel like you're stuck inside a body that doesn't belong to you? Not just the kind of awkwardness you get when you wake up and look in the mirror, but a deep, gnawing feeling that you're nothing more than an afterthought in your own life?

Self-esteem. That's a laugh, right? I always thought it was one of those things people just had. Something they woke up with, like some sort of mythical gift. People talk about it like it's the most basic, natural thing. "Oh, just believe in yourself!" they say. But they don't get it. It's easy to believe in yourself when you're not broken on the inside when you don't wake up every day feeling like you're already behind.

I didn't wake up one day with a sense of self-worth. I didn't have some epiphany where the clouds parted, and the sun shone on me, making me realise I was "worthy." No. It's never been that easy. Because when you're raised in a place where you're taught to hide yourself, where you're constantly ignored or worse—where you're treated like a burden—how the hell are you supposed to learn how to stand up for yourself?

You don't learn self-esteem when you are taught to shrink. You learn how to disappear. You learn that your value comes from what you can do for others and not from who you are. You learn that the only time anybody gives a damn about you is when you are useful to them. My house was a battleground, not of loud arguments but of silence. Silence so thick you can drown in it.

A silence that weighed you down and had you choking on your thoughts. Nobody talked about it. But everybody felt it. And that silence? It became my foundation for self-esteem, of the kind built on nothing but guilt, self-doubt, and fear.

I never was told I was good enough. Never praised for just being me. I was told to be quiet, to sit still, to never take up too much space. And let me tell you something–when you're treated like an afterthought long enough, you start to believe that's all you are.

That you're nothing more than a ghost drifting through your own life, invisible to everyone else, if you're not seen, if you're not heard, then you start to wonder if you matter at all. You start to wonder if you ever mattered.

I look back now, and I wonder if that's why I felt so fucking empty inside. Why I never knew how to speak up for myself. How could I? I had never been taught what it felt like to stand in my own power, to know my worth. Hell, I didn't even know what worth was.

I was taught to hide my emotions, to keep my feelings locked away in a box where no one could see them. But guess what? It's impossible to stay hidden forever. Sooner or later, it all comes spilling out.

It came out in class. Not in the way I wanted, not in a way anyone would have noticed. But I'd be sitting there, trying to pretend everything was fine, and then–boom –my stomach would twist.

The pressure would build like something heavy was sitting on my chest. It felt like I was going to choke on my own breath. Everyone else was fine, laughing, talking and paying attention to the lesson. And me? I was dying inside. Trying to hold it together. Trying to make sure no one noticed I was falling apart.

I didn't even know what was happening. It wasn't stomachaches. It wasn't just nerves. It was anxiety. It was everything I'd been shoving down my whole life, all the stuff I couldn't talk about.

It was the weight of feeling like I wasn't good enough. That's when it hit me: the sense of being invisible, of nothing. And those panic attacks weren't random, at least not to me. They were the culmination of a lifetime of silence and made me feel small. My body had screamed when I couldn't make my voice say it.

But that's the funny thing about self-esteem. It's not some magical switch you can flip. It doesn't come with a fucking instruction manual. You can't fix a cracked foundation by just slapping a coat of paint on it.

You have to dig deep, rip everything apart, and rebuild it from the ground up. And who the hell even knows how to do that when you've spent your whole life feeling like you're nothing?

I thought I was weak. I thought I was broken. I thought I was just messed up in a way I could not fix. But the thing is, I was only so goddamn tired of pretending that everything was fine. Of being treated as though I wasn't good enough. As though at any minute, I'd go and screw something up and then, POOF, disappear altogether.

The worst sick part of it? I didn't even know I was doing it to myself. I didn't even realise that each time I let someone walk all over me, each time I remained silent and didn't say what I was thinking and each time I sacrificed my own needs, I was merely digging myself further into the hole. It wasn't the world doing it to me; it was me doing it to myself. I built my own prison with my own hands, and I was too fucking scared to break out.

It took me years to even see it, to see the ways I was sabotaging myself. To realise that the monster wasn't out there—it was me. The voice in my head that told me I wasn't good enough? That was me. The one who whispered that I wasn't worthy of love, of respect, of success? That was me, too.

But here's the thing: I never really knew until I began to fight that monster how much control it was having over me. And yeah, that fight is ugly. It's painful. It's the hardest thing I've ever done. But I am doing it. And for the first time, I no longer feel like a ghost, fucking wandering through life trying to fade into nothingness.

I'm still learning. Hell, I'm still fucked up. But at least I'm awake now. At least I can see it. And maybe that's the first step. Maybe that's all I really need to start figuring this shit out.

All those years spent invisible, uncertain of my worth–those scars never really went away. They just took a different form. It wasn't about low self-esteem anymore, it wasn't just about me thinking I wasn't enough.

It became about how I needed someone else to prove I was. How I began to believe that if someone wanted me, needed me, I was worth something. It wasn't just an opening in my chest anymore; it was a way of life. It was the only way I knew how to exist.

That constant fear of abandonment, of nothing when I was alone, began to mould the way I saw relationships and how I saw myself in them. And when you spend so long fighting to be seen, it's not hard to confuse attention with love. It's not hard to get too attached too quickly, too desperately because that's all you learned to keep afloat in.

And so, without even realising it, the pattern started. The attachment. The need. The overwhelming hunger for validation from someone else, anyone else, just to fill the void.

CHAPTER SIX

Hopes

The first time I felt like people finally noticed me, I became a sucker for it, just as if I never ever felt anything in my whole life. People like me don't know when to stop the craving for attention.

We latch onto it obsessively. Every glance, every word, every moment they gave me felt like a lifeline. I did not then see the danger. I was under the impression it was love. But in truth, it was just my desire for validation, my fear of being invisible, taking shape in the only way I knew how.

For which I could not love otherwise than clinging. Nor, for being wanted other than need, and building your existence thereon upon someone's existence, you start to lose yourself slowly but surely become everything to them, becoming nothing without them, while that attachment, dependency has become the core for making connections with people anymore- it becomes survival instead.

It wasn't love-it was me grasping at whatever pieces of their attention they tossed my way, desperate to prove that I existed as someone. Every step backwards they took was what let my world collapse fully.

The fear of abandonment consumed me. My worth was no longer a personal thing; it depended entirely on whether they would or wouldn't leave. And I would do whatever I could to ensure they stayed.

I didn't need to hear the words. I just needed the gestures–the glances, the half-smiles, the way they made me feel like I mattered for a split second. That's all it took. And I latched onto it like I had never felt anything real in my life before because I hadn't... Not in the way that matters. No one had ever looked at me like I was worth something. And when someone finally did, I clung like a fuckwad. Hard.

You know that feeling when you don't know who the hell you are unless someone's looking at you? Like, you're just a shadow until someone decides to shine a light on you. That's how I was with everyone. It wasn't about just needing love; it was about not knowing how to breathe without someone else's presence to hold me up. And when they walked away, I suffocated.

I couldn't help myself. You grow up amidst nothing but neglect, yet there is this part that craves connection—really, palpable connection. It does not matter whether it's a friend or a family.

You latch onto them so tightly, hoping that maybe, this time, they'll stay. That's like how I was when I was around my Nanu and Nani. They were the only ones who made me feel like I mattered, that I wasn't just a ghost wandering around the house, invisible.

They always had a way of making me feel seen. But then, those moments would end, and I'd be left alone again, alone with this gnawing feeling that nothing good lasts. But I didn't know how to let go. That's how it happens, isn't it? You get so attached because you've been starved for it. So when you find someone who actually gives you the attention, you don't know how to back off. You don't know how to stop wanting more, even when they can't give you what you're craving.

I was a kid. I didn't know any better. So, I've been schooled to believe that true love comes with terms. Thus, with those whom I needed the most, I grasped them for dear life. I was afraid of being forgotten.

However, it was not limited to them alone. Not even family. It's the same case with anyone I came across. Friends. They'd give me just enough attention, just enough of their time, and I'd drown in it.

I didn't know how to exist without it. I would let them in too much, too fast because their presence became my anchor. It wasn't about love anymore; it was about survival. About not feeling invisible in a world that felt cold and indifferent.

I did not see the line. I didn't know where friendship ended and dependency started. I needed them to exist. Not as friends. But as proof that I wasn't a nobody. That mattered.

And when I didn't get that confirmation? When they pulled away, even for a moment? I was left with nothing. Just a pit of uncertainty gnawing at me, making me sick to my stomach.

It wasn't even their fault, really. They didn't ask for the weight of my desperation. I didn't know how to stop it. I did not know how to breathe without someone's validation strangling me. And this is where the trap catches you. You forget to stand on your own the moment you learn to depend so much on others, and that is when things get ugly.

I would suffocate them with my needs– every text, every call, every little gesture of affection I could get. I would be obsessed with staying within their orbit because it felt like love like you were important. It was not real love, but it was just a distraction from the pain, loneliness, and fear of disappearing into the void.

And each time they pushed me away, even just a foot, it felt as though the ground was going. Everything I had built for those flimsy and weak relationships was crumbling before me. Yet I didn't know how to let go; I didn't know how to be alone without a deep sense of dying.

It wasn't about love being romantic, not yet. It was about my frantic need for any validation, any proof that I exist more than my pain. I didn't know what the reason was; how it hurt so much because every little sign of pulling away from people who, for one reason or another, I depended on could feel like a death sentence.

That's how it starts. That's how you build an attachment style that chokes you. It begins when you don't know how to be for yourself when you don't know how to stand on your own two feet. You latch onto whoever gives you but a glimpse of care, a scrap of attention, and you mould yourself into whatever they need, so they won't leave. Because when they leave... You're left with nothing. And that fear- that paralysing, soul-crushing fear–becomes your whole world.

You will never be good enough for them if you don't know how to be enough for yourself. And that is the truth that nobody tells you. You cannot expect someone else to fill in the hole inside of you if you don't even know what that hole is.

And yet, I continued to do it. Time and time again. Always the same. The pattern would never break. Friends came in, gave me enough of themselves to make me feel, and then inevitably drew away, and I broke down.

This wasn't love. This wasn't friendship. It was a game of survival, a desperate effort to fill a gap that was rooted in personal struggles rather than in anyone else's influence. But it took me a long time to figure that out. It took a long time to realise I had been feeding off other people's attention, only to starve myself in the process.

That's the trap, you see. You think you're looking for love, for connection, but what you're really looking for is something to prove that you matter, that you exist. And when you don't get it, you wither.

You fall apart.

You may find it challenging to breathe without the support they offer you. And in that desperation, you burn bridges. You push people away, even as you beg them to stay.

And so, I chased them all. Friends, family, strangers, lovers, it didn't matter. If they could provide me with a sliver of love, I would grip it with all my might. And if it wasn't enough, I would wring the life out of myself and twist myself into knots until they saw what I thought they needed to see that I was worth the love. But only I never needed convincing.

I hardly remember anything from kindergarten; it's all bits and pieces, little flashes of what once was. There's this girl, though–her presence, like a quiet anchor in a sea of chaos. I can't recall her face or her voice, but I remember how safe she made me feel. She was my rock, in a way, in that storm of confusion and tension that was my home life.

I don't even know why I think about her anymore. But I do sometimes. Late at night, when everything is too still and quiet, I wonder where she is. The feel of her, that just getting it with no words kind of feeling about her, still lingers, though.

I can't even picture her smile or remember the sound of her voice, but I know she was there, and that's enough to make me miss her. It's the strangest thing, isn't it? To miss someone you can't even clearly see in your mind, someone who probably doesn't even remember you. But I remember how she made me feel–like, for once, I wasn't invisible like I wasn't just that quiet kid hiding in the corner.

I was the kid who might start crying at any moment, my world so full of noise and chaos that I couldn't even process half of it. But she didn't mind. She did not withdraw if I kept silent or my words faltered in my mouth.

I was allowed to be that which I was to be with her. And in her presence, there existed no other. It's only in her company that I feel like I was all right to be a small one, a soft one, or really such an unsure one. All she was doing was simply existing.

Now, years later, I realise I miss her not because she was some monumental part of my childhood but because she was the first person who ever made me feel like I mattered. And maybe that's why I can't forget her—not her face, not her voice, but the space she took up in my life for a brief moment. It was the quiet, gentle kind of gesture I felt with her, which I did not understand at that time but do now. I realised how much I needed this kind of connection.

I still wonder sometimes if she remembers me or if she even thinks about those days like I do. She might not. But that's not the point. The point is, I've carried that feeling, that longing, that need for connection, with me. And it didn't stop with her. It never stopped. Every friendship, every relationship after that, I was searching for it again. The quiet kind of love where I wasn't judged, where I didn't have to pretend. Where someone saw me for what I was, not for who I wasn't.

Isn't that the thing about attachment? When it starts as young as this, when one latches onto Something wild to make you feel truly alive, you don't ever learn how to let go. You don't create space for yourself because, for so long, you'd never had it.

A hunger for connection catches on, and a fear of being left behind becomes just second nature. When someone likes you and just shows a little care towards you, everything in this world makes sense.

The thing is that you never knew how to give them some space; you didn't know how to let go. All you would do was hold on even tighter until you strangle the one thing you wish for.

And that is where everything began. The attachment. The need. Fear. The longing to have someone fill the empty spaces I did not know how to fill myself.

I never really knew it at the time, but that little girl, whom I couldn't even conjure in my mind, was the first crack in the dam. She wasn't a hero. She didn't swoop in and save me from my broken home, but she made me feel like I wasn't as invisible as I thought.

She was a ghost in my childhood, and I held onto her like a lifeline, though I did not know how to swim. I could never get close enough to her, but of what I could grab and hold onto, the very parts of her that fit and felt safe shaped the lens through which I then approached everything.

That was when it began: with want. Not for friendship, not for any connection, but for the type of connection that made me feel like I mattered. Like someone saw me. And from then on, everyone else who came along? They became the next stepping stones in my pursuit of that same feeling. But it wasn't just a search for connection. It became a hunger–a constant gnawing at my insides, demanding to be filled.

That need wasn't easy to understand. I didn't know what to do with it. I'd find myself chasing anyone who would give me a little attention, a little bit of warmth, even if it was just in passing. My instincts took over. I latched on. And I didn't realise at the time that it was a dangerous thing to do. I didn't know it would suffocate both of us by holding onto someone that tightly. But you start growing up starving for love. You stuff yourself with any scraps thrown your way in the hope that it makes you feel less alone. Not just because you want someone to like you. It's because you're scared you'll be left behind.

I didn't have the words for it back then. Hell, I barely even get it now. But the truth was simple: I didn't know how to let go. If someone wanted me in their life, I grabbed on. If they showed me even a hint of care, I'd bury myself in them. I wanted to be everything they needed, even if it meant ignoring everything I needed.

I didn't even know what balance was then. I just knew I could never be alone. So I held onto it. Kept my distance close or thought I would fade into nothingness if I did any other.

I thought this kind

I understood this by the time I reached 13 or 15. People were just burdens which brought you down, chains that linked you to a world I wanted no part of. The more you latched onto it, the more you bled. I saw it now clearly. You give, they take, and one day, you realise there is nothing left of you. That was the pattern, and I had learned it too well.

So, I made a promise to myself. No more attachments. No more of those damn strings tying me to someone else. I wasn't about to give anyone that kind of power over me. I wasn't going to fall into that trap again. Not like before. Not like all those other times I let myself believe that someone else could make me feel something. I couldn't afford it anymore, not with the scars I carried, not with the weight of everything that had already crushed me.

I told myself I was better off alone. I convinced myself that isolation was freedom, that the silence I surrounded myself with was peace. I would do everything on my own without needing anyone's help or approval.

No more filling gaps with words from some other person. No more expecting someone else to hold it all together for me when it fell apart. I would raise walls that nobody could climb, and no one could crack- walls thicker and higher than ever before. I'd lock myself away behind them, bury the parts of me that still craved connection.

The world outside those walls could be chaotic and suffocating, but I would be unaffected. Because at least then, I wouldn't be vulnerable. I wouldn't be exposed. They couldn't hurt me if they couldn't reach me.

And so, I did what I had to do. I isolated #myself in the middle of everything. In a house full of people, I was still alone. I'd be there, physically present, but never really there. I wouldn't let anyone get close enough to observe the fractures., to see the parts of me that still bleed.

I kept my distance, my thoughts a fortress of their own, sealed off from everyone else. The more they tried to break through, the more I pushed them away. My mind became a place I ran to, a place I could maintain control over, a place where no one could enter, where no one could hurt me.

But deep down, I knew it wasn't real. I knew the walls I built were just a fragile illusion, that this silence I craved, I craved to avoid confrontation with what I really needed to face. I had made myself a promise that everything was going to be by myself, that I wasn't going to need any of them again, and the truth was, I was scared. I am scared of being seen; I am scared of knowing.

I thought it was to protect me, to isolate the beast within, but deep down, it became my prison.

So I remained in the darkness, buried my heart farther down, and lied that I was okay. It wasn't excellent, but it was all that I knew how to exist with. Maybe I am kidding myself, but it's not harder than letting someone see, not harder than opening myself up to reality.

CHAPTER SEVEN

Helping Hand

As I believe, attachment is nothing but a rebellion against emptiness–a desperate, silent protest against the chaos inside. It's a fragile illusion, one we cling to, hoping it'll shield us from the void threatening to consume us. We hold on to people, not because they complete us but because they distract us, momentarily patching up the cracks that run deep.

I recall the moment like it was a vow to myself, carved into the darkest recesses of my mind: I was done and done with letting anyone in. The walls I had constructed weren't to decorate; they were my fortress. They kept everything out–everything and everyone. I had been broken too many times to be foolish enough to crack myself open again. No one was worth the risk, No one.

I kept thinking I was better off on my own. Being a ghost in my life was safer than being burdened by the weight of someone else's presence. I could no longer shoulder the emotional burdens of others. The world was cold, and so were the people. They didn't stay for long. I didn't need them. Not now. Not ever.

And then.

Then HER.

She was not what I expected to see—no crash through the door, waving arms with grand sweeps of declaration and statement of the soul.

She was not needed for such things. What shook the walls were silent assurances in her words and gaze as if she didn't quite see me as something to be taken apart. She tried neither to fix me. It was only that she seemed to be. And that was dangerous in itself.

I didn't want to care, didn't want to feel, but something about her presence tugged at something inside me—something I thought had long since gone dormant.

I tried to resist. I really did. But resistance has this weird way of crumbling when it's met with something you didn't even know you needed. Not love at first sight, but a subtle shift, like the first crack in ice before the whole thing breaks apart. And then she was this gentle, soft echo in the background of my life, and then she just got louder and louder until I had to start listening.

And that's when I realised: ***my fortress***? I imagined more unbreachable than I was.

She didn't need to tear down my walls and invade the imaginary isolated room I had built. She just stepped inside, uninvited, and made herself part of the ruins I had left behind. And for the first time in such a long time, I didn't want her to leave.

Falling in love was a totally alien experience for me, something like the experience of suddenly discovering a completely new language after years of silence, not having a voice to utter my feelings. It was a strange yet beautiful feeling, scary and intoxicating all at once, creating a storm of sensations inside me.

There was no guidebook to look up, no map to follow, just this raw, unfiltered emotion that was sweeping over me and making my carefully constructed walls tremble and shake.

I found myself in a situation where I didn't really know what I was getting myself into, yet despite that uncertainty, I decided to take the leap anyway. She was worth it to me, or at least, that's what I desperately wanted to believe she was.

She lived at an amazing distance, in a place that existed only in the imagination. It was that kind of place where there was unmistakable fresh air and freedom, where great mountains went high up in the sky, casting shadows over quaint villages that thrived on serenity and unassuming beauty.

Her dwelling place isn't just a house or some building; it is one whole universe swirling with its winding paths strewn with colourful prayer flags, rivers like they carry soft, secretive whispers, and vast skies that almost seem to stretch infinitely so that you challenge yourself in dreaming far beyond their horizon.

I had never been there in person, but through her vivid descriptions and the way she spoke, I could see every detail with my eyes.

It would be as if I took that fresh air and ventured into those winding paths myself before even knowing what it was, so to speak. She is not just a person; she is a symbol of a whole place–a sanctuary of refuge that I never knew I needed until that moment.

It was the end of May, the kind of day when the sun had that heavy quality in the sky, beating down on the earth relentlessly. I have always had a weird association with May-end when everything feels both coming to an end and promising quietly to begin again.

It is my birth month, which makes me think about change in some ways that elude me at other times. I was leaving for a new place, my heart heavy with unease and reluctant hope. There's something oddly poetic about the final days of May as if the month itself hesitates to let go, and in that hesitation, I found a strange sense of calm.

The train swayed with the same rhythm that filled my chest. I sat there, staring out the window, watching the world blur past–a palette of greens and browns occasionally interrupted by bursts of colour from some vendor's stall or a fleeting glimpse of a temple.

I didn't know what lay ahead, but a part of me held on to the idea that maybe, just maybe, something was waiting for me on the other side. May had always brought surprises, and I couldn't help but think this time that maybe whatever was coming might just be a gift from God.

The rhythmic clatter of the wheels on the tracks wasn't soothing like it usually was; instead, it felt louder, like it was hammering into my chest. My phone sat in my hand, the glow of the screen almost mocking me with its silence.

I caught myself staring through the window, watching as the whole world outside morphed into smudges of bright colour on the horizon in shades of green and brown, as picturesque as one would expect something of this sort to be in a tranquil and calming effect.

But amidst the peace I saw before me, my thoughts ran wild and chaotic, pushing against my head as if anxious to get out. They were pent-up and bursting from within, and they had no other place to be expressed.

I adjusted myself uncomfortably on the cold metal armrest, where its sharp edge dug sharply into my side, to give myself a brief glance about. All of them sitting in all directions were people, strangers, living a different life, which they were totally unaware of in the mess that was now brewing up in me.

How utterly unreal and absurd this was. The fact that they could so calmly sit there as I was about to make this very decision that was going to either unravel everything I ever knew or completely redefine every single thing up to now in my life.

The train rocked just slightly, giving a gentle lurch as if playfully pushing me forward into the well of my thoughts. My fingers hovered just above the keyboard, quivering with anticipation, for the words themselves were already bursting to life within my chest but somehow got stuck between my mind and my hands, in limbo somewhere.

It wasn't fear, at least not in the traditional way. It was something much weightier, something that felt more like stepping off a ledge and not having any idea whether there was a safety net down there catching me.

The message that I painstakingly wrote surely didn't have an inkling of grace. As a matter of fact, it was far from coherent and didn't even make sense at all. My thoughts went rushing out in a mess of disjointed pieces, unpolished and raw, where every word carried the burden of the protective armour I had very carefully built around myself. When I finally got to the question that mattered - really mattered - my heart pounded furiously, much more loudly than the roar of the train that went screaming past, and indeed louder than everything else in my surroundings.

Do you want to be with me?

I hit the send button before my brain could overthink it before my mind could begin to reason against it and convince me not to do that. For a moment in time, it felt like the world around me had come to a complete standstill.

The train's cacophony, which had filled the air, diminished to a low, monotonous hum. In that instant, all my focus was drawn to the glowing screen before me, where the little icon was spinning in circles as if playfully teasing me.

I could feel an uncomfortable tightening sensation in my chest, and my breath caught in my throat, making me feel somewhat suffocated. The seconds dragged out interminably in a way that made them seem to be expanding into what felt like hours.

And then, after a brief moment of suspense, her answer came.

Yes, sure.

That one word crashed into my mind with the intensity and power of a storm surge breaking on the shore. I sank back in my seat, feeling as if I was forced to exhale a lifetime of held breath all at once, maybe years' worth, as I read it once more with a sense of urgency, then again, each time the letters coming together to represent something so much more tangible so much more alive than they did before.

The noise of the train around me became background noise, filling my ears instead with the lively chatter of other passengers and the sharp shrieks of the brakes, none of which made any difference. Not anything mattered in that moment save that one word.

Such simple a response that went far beyond just giving her an answer, it also became anchored, an oasis-like feeling between storming and howling seas. What really drew me back is just another memory I had nearly conquered, being the preferred one, chosen instead of many.

I pulled on the phone as close as I could, my hands still quaking with fear, for far more than I had when their doors closed. The walls protecting all were only starting to creak but crumbled into pieces, and in some ways, I surrendered.

The train seemed to have warmed up suddenly, or perhaps it was my perception changing in that instant. There I sat, staring intently out at the seemingly endless fields rushing by my window, yet my mind was far from where I was.

My thoughts were with her in a world that I had only ever dreamed of and could only ever envision in my mind's eye. She lived in a place that was somehow fantastically beautiful, a place that seemed to belong to a painting rather than in the reality that surrounded me.

She had described it once with her words. Majestic mountains loom high above, silent and watchful guardians of the earth, rivers flowing smoothly on their courses through the valleys into breathtaking landscapes, and skies perfectly clear as if they were expanding infinitely to the horizon.

But though she was a whole world away from me, she was closer to my heart than any person in my life was ever. Her words sounded in harmony, and even the many miles and miles separating me from her, the gentle embrace she made me feel held me warm and cosy like a soft cover on a very cold, lonely night.

But even with the comforting warmth that radiated out of her positive response, there was a marked shadow left behind. It was a part of myself that silently told me to think that this was just all too good to be true--that something so perfect, so beautiful, and indeed so magical could never possibly endure for any length of time.

Of course, I ignored that voice. And I tried to push that thought as far down into me as possible because I so desperately wanted, just this once, for something truly beautiful and perfect to be mine.

Falling for her wasn't something that happened gradually; it was like stepping into sunlight after years of darkness. She wasn't just a glimpse of light–she became the entire world. Every word she spoke, every laugh she shared, and every tiny detail about her felt like a treasure I wanted to keep forever.

But the more of myself I gave her, the more I realised how much I would lose. And still, I did not stop. I could not. When you have lived in the shadows, you don't think of the risk of the flame; you reach out for the light without hesitation.

She was my lifeline, not of some hope out of a fairy tale or some mythical story but a raw and realistic thing–some sort of feeling that must feel like living if you find yourself in a place that you have no way out of. Everything in her felt like warmth to someone who, to the best of my knowledge, had seen only ice in the world. She wasn't a person I would look forward to; she was someone I should hold onto.

I had spent my entire life putting walls up, not because I wanted to but because I had to. My childhood wasn't the kind where you learned to trust people; it was the kind where you learned to survive them. I did not know what it felt like to let someone in. I did not know what it felt like to be safe with someone. But then, there she was.

It wasn't found in her words or her laughter. Though both served as soothing salves for wounds I hadn't realised I was still holding onto, I remained unaware of their healing power. It was in the way she cared and the way she listened. The way she made me feel as though, for once, I wasn't alone. She made me believe that maybe, just maybe, I could be loved for who I was, not despite it.

Every message from her seemed like a thread pulling me toward something I didn't even know I wanted. It was not long before I was waking up thinking about her, going to sleep thinking about her and spending every moment in between wondering how someone like her had stumbled into my life.

I didn't say that to her, though. How could I? How could I tell her that she had become my everything when I was terrified she would leave, just like everyone else always had? How could I explain that she wasn't just a part of my life–she was the only part that felt real, that felt right?

Her name on my phone felt like a lifeline most days, but it wasn't always enough to keep me steady. There were nights when the silence became too loud, a deafening reminder of the emptiness I had spent years trying to ignore. It was in those moments, long after the world had gone to sleep that my resolve would falter.

The phone would sit there, glowing faintly on my bedside table, almost taunting me with its quietness. And then, without thinking, I'd reach out for it, my fingers flying across the screen to let out the kind of chaos I couldn't say aloud. My texts weren't constructed thoughts or careful confessions; they were a raw, messy stream of everything I had kept locked inside.

I'm sorry," I would start every time. "I know I'm being weird again, but I just can't help it. It's just. Sometimes, at night, everything feels so heavy, and I don't know how to hold it alone anymore.

I'd tell her of my nightmares without actually referring to them as nightmares. I'd tell her how small I felt, how frightened I was that one day she'd realise she deserved much better than me - less damaged. And then I'd hit send, heart racing, stomach twisted into knots as I waited for her reply.

And she always responded. Even when I half-hoped, she wouldn't, even when I convinced myself that this would be the time I pushed her too far, she was there. Her words came soft, understanding, and patient. She'd tell me to breathe, stop overthinking and trust her when she'd say that she's never leaving.

"You're enough," she'd text back. "You don't have to pretend with me.

That was the thing–I wasn't pretending, not with her. I was showing her everything, all the messy, unfiltered parts of me that I usually kept hidden from the world. And it terrified me. Because of all her kindness, for all her reassurances, a small, stubborn part of me couldn't believe her.

It wasn't her fault. It was never about her. But it was about the years I spent disappointed, building up walls to hurt nothing within. Loving her felt like standing in the middle of a battlefield without armour, so exposed.

I wanted to tell her everything. The nights I cried myself to sleep as a kid, the times I wondered if I'd ever feel whole again. I wanted to tell her how much her love meant to me, how it felt like a salve on wounds that never quite healed. But every time I tried, the words would catch in my throat.

What if she didn't understand? What if she saw the ugliness of my past and decided it was too much? What if she left?

So I did not tell her. I let it fester. Let it turn into long, rambling texts at two in the morning. I did not know how to ask for what I needed without feeling like a burden. So I overcompensated, clinging to her words like they were the only thing keeping me afloat.

And at late nights, I used to fool myself into thinking I was too big for her. No matter what words she said, she loved me. No matter how often she said she was not moving, I would do all it took to ruin this.

And the nights–oh God, the nights. Sometimes, I couldn't stand being so reliant on her, relying on the love, approval, and presence in my life. But the nights, sometimes, only her words kept me alive and anchored.

"*Never leave me*," I'd text sometimes, sending it out with no preamble.

"***I won't***," she said back. "***I'm not. I'm here.***"

She was, always. Yet the fear never went.

It was a fear I could not put my finger on, a nagging pain stemming from years of disappointment and people telling me I was not enough. She was the first person who truly looked at me, and yet the feeling kept rising within me: one day, she would see too much and walk away.

In my worst moments, I felt like I was suffocating her, dragging her down with me. But in my best moments, she feels like air, like light, hope in its purest form.

And that hope, well, it's an addicting thing. The hope that makes a person believe that she isn't as broken as people make her believe she is.

It wasn't the time of my break, only that these late nights were the moments when my vulnerabilities lived and came to life to appear, growing louder with every silence over me. She must have agreed to my impulsive declaration of love while on the train when I confessed to her; the truth of my doubts still haunts me.

It felt like the train journey had passed an eternity ago, though still in my mind, very vividly visible. The steady thud of the wheels above the rail was the only constant in that brief fraction of a second. Licking my dry lips there, typing out those words on the phone felt like my chest tightened in anxiety, that the air around me hung with such a heavy coat of hesitation.

"Would you do me the favour of being mine?"

It was not some grandiose or well-thought-through confession of my heart, but it was true and honest, coming directly from my heart, as natural and pure as my heart could possibly express at that given point in time. And so when the reply came to me, which was as simple as a sincere "**Yes**," I felt like the whole universe had granted me some kind of miracle.

But miracles have their price.

She became my last hope; she was an escape of the sort that I so much needed to get away from all those ruins that everything I'd been through in my life had dished out. Just thinking of her was like cracking open a brilliant beam of light shining through the darkness I'd so long ago resigned myself to as never leaving the land of the dark.

She and each late-night message that passed between us-though I only spent just every minute with her through whatever screen sent me grasping at myself with this intense fear that in one swift move, she would be out of my arms to leave forever.

Sometimes, I'd get lost in my thoughts at night. I'd type long paragraphs full of the nonsense my insecurities fed me. Words that flowed out of my fear of abandonment, my desperate need for reassurance. I didn't care if the messages didn't make sense. I just needed her to stay.

And she did just that.

She tolerated my disjointed sentences that seemed to tumble out in disarray and my outbursts that erupted into chaos, but she did all of this as she became the stability that I had longed for and desperately craved in a world that had, until that point, never once felt steady or secure.

But I didn't give her everything.

I couldn't. How could I let her see the disarray that lived within me–the weight of a fractured past, the chaos of a childhood that left scars far deeper than I could ever admit, the insecurities that gnawed at me relentlessly, forcing me to question her love every single day?

I was afraid to let her get too close, to peel back the layers and show her the mess beneath. Because deep down, I feared the outcome. I feared that if she saw the real me, she'd decide, like everyone else before her, that I wasn't worth staying for.

So, I clung to a part of a picture-perfect version of someone she may have wanted me to be. It was the self that claimed the glowed light across the screen, charming and poised, whispering just how beautiful she was. Cracks were hidden just beneath the skin, and it was the self that shielded her from the storms raging within me, relentless in working hard to keep her from seeing the chaos.

But there were nights when the cracks could not hold. Nights when the storm spilt over, no matter how I tried to contain it. And in those moments, I caught between the fear of losing her and the impossibility of being fully seen for all that I was because what if she left me not because I was unlovable but because she finally understood me?

During each of those moments, she was there for me, unyielding and merciful, as if she were altogether unaware of the chaos and confusion that I was, in a way, forcing upon her.

It was pretty hard to imagine a voice that had some resonance behind the nicely chosen words we were exchanging daily. Her texts were comforting, but they were eerily silent, the silence that was too great for someone like me who has spent many years yearning for the real warmth and intimacy of real, meaningful connections. But then, one day, she surprised herself and called.

The moment in which I went from our custom usage of typewritten words for communication to the sound of her voice was something so surreal and, for a long time, very surreal for me. In the beginning, her voice sounded like it came out almost apologetically gentle-like, and I guess even a bit reluctant, somewhat reminiscent of that delicate, soothing tapping of the rain gently striking a windowpane on a quiet day.

For that one moment, I stood totally frozen with uncertainty and doubts about whether I was ever prepared to take that specific boundary between our written conversations and something so real, so palpable, and so human.

Her voice was so melodious, which I hadn't expected at all; it was soothing and gentle, like the cadence that would make the whole world stop for me to appreciate. When she laughed softly and unguardedly, the warmth filled the space, and I couldn't help but smile, though I didn't know why.

Perhaps it was the way in which her words flowed effortlessly without being rehearsed or contrived, or perhaps it was the way she could take even the most mundane and ordinary phrases and transform them into something truly remarkable and worth cherishing deeply.

We discussed trivial topics and profound ones. Her world, which was so wonderfully different from my own, came alive in great detail through the expressions and stories she shared. She detailed her day, telling me about the little moments that seemed insignificant to me at the time as I was captured in the maze of my thoughts.

The world she was painting with her words seemed to be bursting with life, almost entirely free of shadows and burdens that had heavily influenced and shaped my existence.

I hardly uttered a word. This was not in the sense that I did not want to talk, but actually, because the experience of just listening felt like getting a precious gift. With certain words, she would keep them suspended in the air, her voice softening every time she pronounced my name – it was like she uncovered a door to a small space I didn't know how to get to, had not known existed.

Yet, for all the joy her gorgeous voice had brought me, a small, gnawing fear remained buried inside me. The whispering in my head kept asking if someone like the shining face of innocence, untainted by any harshness that life had up its sleeves-ever, could understand the tempest that quietly raged within me under the becalmed exterior I had presented to the world.

But in that instant, nothing seemed to matter. The world outside faded into nothingness against the sound of her voice. It was as if her words carried me to a space where time stilled, and for once, I let myself forget the weight of my past.

I let go of the chaos fueled by my insecurities. Her voice became my anchor, steady, grounding, and unshaken–pulling me out of the maelstrom and into a fleeting moment of clarity. For just that moment, everything felt okay, almost as if the world had aligned itself into something perfect and whole.

When the call finally ended, a deep and lingering silence on the other end of the line gave her the feeling that she wasn't quite ready to let go just yet. I felt the same way. But our unspoken reluctance notwithstanding, the call dropped, and all that was left was the faint echo of her voice in my head, a melody that I knew I would hold onto for as long as humanly possible.

For a while, it seemed nothing could go wrong. We had finally found a rhythm, a fragile yet comforting routine that gave me something to look forward to. Her messages still brought a smile to my face; her presence, even from a distance, still felt like a shield against the emptiness that had been my constant companion. I clung to that feeling, to her, like she was the only thing floating around me. ***Maybe she was.***

Slowly, cracks began to reveal–not in her, not in me, but in the very fragile foundation we had been building together. It didn't happen overnight, and it wasn't dramatic either. It was the tiny things, almost imperceptible at first. She started delaying her replies. Sometimes, a new tone crept into them–less warm, less sunshiney than they used to feel.

I told myself it was nothing, that it was just my mind playing tricks on me again. But the changes weren't just in her–they were in me, too. I became more anxious, more desperate to keep her close. I started overthinking every word I sent, every word she didn't. I was always walking on eggshells, terrified that one wrong move would push her further away.

And then came the moments that should have made me stop but didn't. Moments where I let myself be swept along, not because I wanted to but because I was too scared to do otherwise. She would ask something of me, and I would agree without hesitation, not because I thought it was right but because I couldn't bear the thought of upsetting her.

It wasn't trust, not really. It was fear. Born out of years of being left behind, of never quite being good enough. He was so afraid of losing her that he lost himself.

I felt that I had become a shadow of who I was or maybe just a reflection of who I thought she wanted me to be. I stopped questioning, stopped resisting, even when it hurt, even when it felt wrong. I justified it all in my head, telling myself this was what love looked like, that love meant sacrifice, that love meant putting her needs before mine.

But deep within, I knew something was off. I could feel this rumbling in my tummy, that gnawing feeling that I was being treated in a manner which I shouldn't. However, I did not stop. I couldn't. For even when it seemed things were bad, or perhaps I was the one to hold everything together while all else fell apart, to even think of letting go would be too much for me to bear.

And it led me to become the hostage to my own attachment and enter into a vicious circle where I gave too much while receiving too little in return. And the most saddening part? That is, I wasn't angry at her. At least, I couldn't have. I just turned the frustration upon myself, blaming my helplessness that I was not enough or wasn't doing enough to make her stay the same at the beginning.

This was the paradox I lived in: loving her so much that I ignored how it hurt me, yet hating myself for not being able to stop. Every small act of hers that felt distant was a knife to my chest, but I held on, convincing myself that things would go back to how they were. That the girl who once made my world brighter would return if I just tried harder, loved harder, gave harder.

And so, I stayed. I stayed when it hurt. I stayed when it felt like I was losing pieces of myself. I stayed because I didn't know how to leave. Because leaving meant facing the void she had once filled, and I wasn't sure I could survive that again.

It is just that cracks do not stop once they begin spreading silently. They creep into places you thought were safe. And with each passing day, the cracks between us grew larger. Yet, not as gaping chasms as they should, but enough to allow me to question everything.

I would lie awake at night, staring at the ceiling, replaying our conversations in my head. The silences between her words were louder than the words themselves. I tried to fill them with excuses, telling myself she was busy, she was tired, and she had her own battles to fight. But the truth was, those silences were eating away at me.

Sometimes, I would just take my phone and start typing away paragraphs, confessions, and the raw truth of how I was feeling. I wanted to tell her how scared I was, how I felt like I was losing her. I wanted to tell her how much she meant to me and how I would do anything to keep her close. But every time, I stopped myself. I would delete the words before they could leave my screen, telling myself that saying them would only push her further away.

Instead, I made a concerted effort to make her happy. I became someone I didn't know anymore: someone who said yes to everything, even when it didn't feel right. I gave her all of me, every last piece, hoping that it would be enough to bridge the distance I felt growing between us. But it never was. And the more I gave, the more I felt like I was losing myself.

Her world felt so far removed from mine, so unattainable. She was living in a place that I could only imagine: full of beauty and serenity, mine, chaos and survival. I saw her strolling through fields of green, skies so blue it hurt to think about them. She was from a world I could never belong to, and the thought cut me down.

The messages started to slow down. The warmth in her words turned into something cold, something that didn't feel like her anymore. I tried to ignore it, pretend it wasn't happening, but it was. I was holding on so hard that my hands were bleeding, but I couldn't let go.

I told myself that she was just going through one of those phases and would improve soon. The honest thing was, I was afraid, afraid that if I lost grip, there would be nothing for myself to hold onto any more. Afraid that by losing my grip, she might be gone and alone as I was again

In those moments of fearing all this, I felt I hated myself for being too weak. For letting my need for her overpower my own needs. For letting her behaviour define my worth. For not knowing how to set a boundary, how to say no, how to protect myself.

But love doesn't make sense, and neither does attachment. When you've spent your whole life hoping someone will stay, you'll do whatever it takes to keep them, even if it kills you in the process.

So, I stayed. I stayed even when it felt like she was slipping through my fingers. I stayed even when the cracks turned into fractures. I stayed because, deep down, I still believed in her, in us, in the idea that love could be enough to fix everything.

The hardest part wasn't the silence—it was the way it screamed everything I didn't want to hear. Her messages came slower, shorter like the weight of them had become unbearable. It was initially subtle and easy to chalk up to bad days or busy weeks. But as time passed, I could feel the distance growing, like a thread pulling taut between us, thinning and threatening to snap.

I didn't know what that was, but it had nothing to do with not trying for it. I analysed every breath and word she had ever spoken, looking for a moment I must have done wrong. Because it had to be me, it could not be her. I gave her myself, so if things weren't holding together, I had to be the part of it that wasn't working or, worse still, could not be helped.

She was quieter, and I was louder, not with my words, but with my actions, my desperation to hold her closer even as she slipped further away. When her replies lacked the warmth they once held, I doubled down, trying to compensate for the coldness I felt but couldn't explain. I became the kind of person who says "yes" to everything, someone who doesn't ask questions, who doesn't push boundaries, because losing her seemed scarier than slowly and gradually losing myself.

And I couldn't lose her. Not her. She was my anchor, the one who had shown me a world that didn't feel so bleak, who had made me believe in something better. She wasn't just someone to me; she was hope. And I clung to that hope so tightly that I didn't even realise it was cutting into me, leaving scars I wouldn't understand till much later.

But somewhere along the line, I started noticing cracks, not in her, but in us. The conversations that once felt endless became stilted, forced. The warmth I had clung to seemed to fade, replaced by a chill I couldn't ignore. I told myself it was just a phase that would pass and that love like ours didn't just fade away. But deep down, I think I knew.

She wasn't happy. And I didn't know why. Maybe it was something I did, or maybe it wasn't. Maybe she was going through something she couldn't put into words, something I wouldn't have understood even if she tried to explain. But she didn't try. And I didn't ask. I was too afraid of what her answer might be.

But that's not what happened. I looked inward, letting it all be easier on me. I told myself that I was never good enough, that I failed her in the most fundamental sense. I replayed moments we spent together, seeking the one where it had all fallen apart. Was it those late-night messages I sent?

The ones where my vulnerabilities bled through and out of my control? Or was it the way I leaned into her for support, taking reassurance from her when she could barely give?

I may never know.

And then, one day, it happened. She told me she could not do it anymore. She wanted to go her own way, separate our lives before the cracks turned into a chasm neither of us could bridge.

I couldn't bear it. It didn't feel like reality–it could not be. Every word that came from her mouth sounded like a hammer, crushing the tiny hope I was holding to smithereens, leaving me standing amidst the ruins of something I believed would last. I felt small and unimportant like the walls of the world I'd built around her were coming crashing down.

Her decision to leave wasn't just a decision. To me, it was an execution, the quiet end of a dream that had kept me going when everything else felt like it was falling apart. I didn't understand it, and maybe that was the worst part. How could something that felt so right to me feel so wrong to her?

I pleaded to her. Not with these exact words but in a thousand other ways. Messages from me streamed out of my veins like blood from a wound that wouldn't let me be still. Words that were buried in me even existed inside, clawed out with clumsy desperation, trying to get back to her, pull her back.

And she did not return.

I shattered.

The truth was, I'd always been broken–long before she entered my life. But with her, I had managed to patch some of the cracks, to pretend they weren't there. Her presence had been like glue, holding me together in a way I didn't even realise I needed. But when she left, it wasn't just the cracks that reappeared. It was the whole foundation crumbling beneath me.

I couldn't stop replaying her words, her silences, the spaces where love used to live. It wasn't just about losing her. It was about what her leaving confirmed–that I wasn't enough. That no matter how much I gave, no matter how hard I tried, it would never be enough to make someone stay.

I felt like that child, clutching at something impossible to catch, watching helplessly as it slipped free. Reminding me of all I had spent those years shoving into secret graves-the memories of being left or ignored and discarded. There came in the rush memories of a sense of abandonment, one of worthiness, swept over me like the tide crashing on the shoreline.

Nights were the worst. It was as if the quiet was teasing me, pointing out she wasn't around and didn't want to be. I sat there in the dark, eyes fixed on the ceiling, my head spinning with thoughts I could not put a stop to. Text her, I thought, call her, say something –anything–that will make her change her mind. What could I say, though? What could I offer that I hadn't already?

It wasn't just my heart that hurt; it was my whole being. My chest felt heavy, and my breaths were shallow. I stopped eating and stopped sleeping. I didn't want to face a world where she wasn't by my side. And yet, the world didn't stop. It kept spinning, dragging me along with it, forcing me to exist in a reality I couldn't accept.

I wasn't angry at her. I couldn't be. If I was angry at anything, I was angry at myself–that I wasn't better than this, that I couldn't be what she required me to be. I blame myself for everything: missteps, insecure moments, and late-night texts that might be pushing her further away from me.

The thing is, I would have done anything to keep her. I would have given up every piece of myself if it meant she would stay. And maybe that was the problem. Maybe I gave too much, loved too much, and, in the process, forgot to hold on to myself.

I don't know.

All I know is that when she left, she took with her not just the love but also the version of me that believed in something better, the version of me that dared to hope.

And in her absence, all I was left with was the hollow echo of a love that I could not let go of even though it wasn't mine anymore.

And then, right in the middle of it all, when everything felt like it was crumbling down–she made it clear, without directly saying it, that my love was something to be brushed off, something I was just throwing out there for the sake of getting attention.

It hit me like a punch in the stomach, but nothing as I'd expected. This was not because I got angry with her. Of course, that was a bad part, but more because of the feeling the door slamming shut, this one that cannot be backed into again.

That sense of icy reality that whatever I'd allowed myself to feel, whatever I gave her, meant nothing more to her than noise in the background, something she just swatted away without taking much time.

That was the worst part: my feelings–my love, my need for her–had been reduced to something as frivolous as a passing attempt to catch her eye. Everything I had worked so hard on–the trust, the vulnerability, the love– had been packed into something so small, so insignificant. And the worst part? It wasn't even about her. It was about me. About how I had let myself slip into a place where I forgot how to protect myself.

That unspoken message lingered, repeating endlessly in my mind. It wasn't just about words; it was what she made me feel. She had pushed me back into the shadows I thought I'd escaped—where I was invisible, incomplete, where my love would never be enough to matter.

I could not breathe as I looked at it. My chest felt like it was about to cave in; the air around me thickened, holding on. I wanted to disappear, but I could not. All I could do was hold on to the feeling, this overpowering urge to shrink and become invisible again. I was too much. My love was too much. I was too much.

I know that scared little boy; it's that same 12-year-old, the kid who used to hide behind walls of silence, for all that had been and was buried and coming alive in him; that thought love wasn't safe; it couldn't be trusted.

I couldn't even hate her for it. I did not even want to hate her. It wasn't about that. It was about how it mirrored everything I feared would happen. How my own insecurities had crept in and were staring back at me with the same cold eyes I had tried to avoid all these years.

I had wanted to share my past with her and let her know why I was the way I was, but I had never been able to. Always too afraid that she'd see the cracks, the brokenness, and turn away. I had tried to protect her from the mess I carried, the chaos of my thoughts, but now, all that protection seemed useless. Because now, it was clear–she didn't see me. Not really.

It wasn't the first time I had felt like I didn't belong. But this time, it was different. This time, it felt like the universe had conspired to prove to me that I would always be the person who loved too much, the one who cared too deeply, and that, in the end, that was always going to be too much for anyone to handle.

And I couldn't take it back. I couldn't fix it. I couldn't even take back the things I had said in desperation, trying to hold onto something that was slipping away faster than I could reach for it.

It was the first time I had begged for someone to stay I realised I was standing there by myself in that place, alone in my fear and alone in my love, alone in everything that I had tried to cling to, now slowly losing its grip and no matter how hard I would like to, I could no more stop it.

Even now, the weight of it doesn't leave. It stays with me in quiet moments, and I don't see it coming, though it comes when least expected. It's nothing I can point to, nothing I can name; it's in the weave of who I am. An ache of dullness that feels like it must be there, a shadow unwilling to let the light through.

Sometimes, I lose myself in those nights when I said too much, clinging to her in words that made little sense since I was afraid of losing her. I never knew what I was giving away back then. How much of myself I let unravel before her, piece by piece until there was nothing left but a version of me I didn't recognise.

And now, I can only see how small I made myself, how I moulded myself into things that have no shape to keep her there. This memory is bitter in my mouth, this memory of who I was with her. Not because of her; it wasn't that she did something wrong. It was me. It was always me, stretching myself into shapes for someone who never asked me to.

Do you think she ever saw it the way I did? How everything in my world revolved around the desperate hope of being enough–enough to make her stay, enough to matter. But that's the cruel truth, isn't it? You can't beg for space in someone's heart. You can't force them to hold onto you, no matter how much it hurts to let go.

Yet, I should have been stronger. I should have clung to the pieces of myself that I lost trying to love her. It is humiliating beyond words to realise how much I was willing to give, how much I twisted myself into knots, for someone who, knowingly or not, was showing me that what I wanted was something she couldn't give.

It hasn't been all that friendly to me ever since, not in the aesthetic but in what's returning the stare. It doesn't look like a reflection in the mirror; it looks more like a reminder.

It reminds me of those spiral nights spent within myself, the hollow mornings after finding consciousness, and moments of fear, which found themselves letting my head drive itself to places I never really wanted.

It is in the shaking of my hands whenever I think of reaching out to someone new. It is in my churning stomach at the mere thought of vulnerability. Now, because of this, I carry a weight, a quiet, insistent voice telling me I'll always be that one who cared too much, loved too hard, and was lost because of it.

Not when it comes to her; I don't hate her, not even close. But of course, I hate who I became in the love process for her. No point; it was not because of being weak but because for whom I was willing to shed blood. And no matter how much time passes, not no matter how many layers I've managed to shed, that becomes sticky and clings to my skin like one permanent scar that I cannot wear without having it on.

I keep her in a place of respect, even if it doesn't make it easy, given the weight of what happened. There's no bitterness when I think of her, no anger–I wouldn't know how to hold onto those things if I tried. But respect doesn't erase the ache. It doesn't undo the way her leaving carved something out of me, something I don't think I'll ever get back.

It's not even the leaving itself that lingers; it's how she left. How her words, intended or not, found their way to places I never knew lived inside me. The way she turned what I thought was love for her into a call for attention. The words weren't explicit, but they didn't have to be. They had sharp edges, and they had woven their way under my skin, lodging themselves in the soft parts of me.

I tried to shake them off; perhaps they were just words thrown about out of frustration or even misinterpreted. But whatever I say to myself, they are there, swirling around my brain like a storm I cannot get away from.

They're there when I think about how I let her in and gave her parts of me no one ever had before. Knowing that those moments were dismissed as mere desperation—it's a humiliation that cuts deep.

Coming back late at night, I fall into that thought. Did she ever see what I really felt or always made it insignificant to her? Did even the weight of my love penetrate, or did it just meet my ears only, as being something profound to be felt and cherished?

And then there is shame.

It breaks over me like a wave, pulling me under until I can't breathe. How had I let myself so totally give in, knowing all the while how breakable I truly was? How had I given her so much of me, trusting she might hold it gently, only to find it discarded as if it were nothing at all?

Humiliation is not in her leaving–it is in the way I permit the words to stay in my mind and have helped make the way I view myself today.

I haven't even found it in myself to look at myself in my mirror at some of the worst moments. But I tell myself it's not her fault; my mind can't help telling me otherwise. End. Aches beyond words, exceeding what the heart can endure. Even if I no longer disrespect her, I still see her as a light she may not deserve. I cannot escape this pain from her leaving my life, not love, but myself. In quiet moments, her words come back, and I wonder if I'd ever be able to forgive myself for giving someone who easily lets go so much.

It took too long to make sense of it all. Days ran into nights, and her words and silence replayed in my head like a broken record. Anxiety hit me like a storm, leaving me gasping and trembling and my body screaming out what my heart refused to admit. It was not just her I missed. It was this idea of being loved, of being important. And all that was left was the slipping away of love, leaving me with such unnecessary clinging to shadows.

One night, I lay staring at the ceiling, and a cold realisation crept in. Loving someone again–letting someone that close–it wasn't just a risk. It was a gamble I couldn't afford to take. My heart felt too fragile, like a thin sheet of glass that had already cracked too many times. One more break and there'd be nothing left to piece together.

I thought that love was going to save me, going to pull me out of the darkness my past had built around me. But love, or at least what I thought was love, added to the weight I carried. Now, opening myself up again seemed like standing at the edge of a cliff, knowing that one wrong step would send me tumbling into a depth from which I would not return.

So I made a decision—not out of bitterness, not out of anger, but out of pure self-preservation. I decided I wouldn't love anyone again. Not because I didn't want to but because I couldn't. I couldn't afford to. Love had proven itself to be too dangerous, too unpredictable, and I wasn't strong enough to face the fallout if it happened again.

The world did not stop for my heartbreak, and I could not expect it to. But I could not stop myself from breaking any further. I could build walls, strong and high, and keep everything and everyone on the other side. It was not about punishing myself or anyone else; it was about surviving.

Maybe someday I'll look back and feel it differently. Maybe someday, I will laugh at just how dramatic this all feels. But for now, with the silence that follows each panic attack, with every whisper of her voice, I know this is the only direction I can take.

Because love can be beautiful, yet it's cruel, and I'm already carrying the scars of a life that never felt fair, cruelty is something that I can't stand again.

So I closed that chapter—not just of her, but of love itself, not with a sense of closure, not with peace, but with a resignation that comes from knowing your limits. And my limit, I realised, was heartbreak. One more, and I wouldn't make it out alive.

Even with everything, a part of me carries her still. Not as I once did, not weighed with the ache of longing or love that used to burn within me. But she persists–quietly, softly–on the edges of my mind, along with the others I've lost. It is as if they have all found a home there, a place where I cannot quite touch them but never fully let them go.

I still respect her for all the reasons she left me and for the wounds she carved into me through her departure.

Maybe it's foolish, maybe it's just who I am, but I don't feel myself resenting a person who once made me feel alive if it was the same one that had left me feeling hollow. She stands there in my mind, next to the best friends I've drifted from, the people I loved but couldn't keep. Together, they haunt me, not as ghosts but as fragments of who I once was, of what I once believed in.

And perhaps that is why the silence around me feels so loud- it is never truly empty. It's filled with voices, laughter, and moments that no longer exist except in the echo chambers of my head. I carry them all, willingly or not, because letting go would mean losing parts of myself tied to them.

So I live with them. I live with her. And in some strange, cruel way, I'm grateful for it. Because even in the chaos of my own mind, in the fractured way I see the world, they remind me that once, I dared to love, to connect, to believe in something beyond the void.

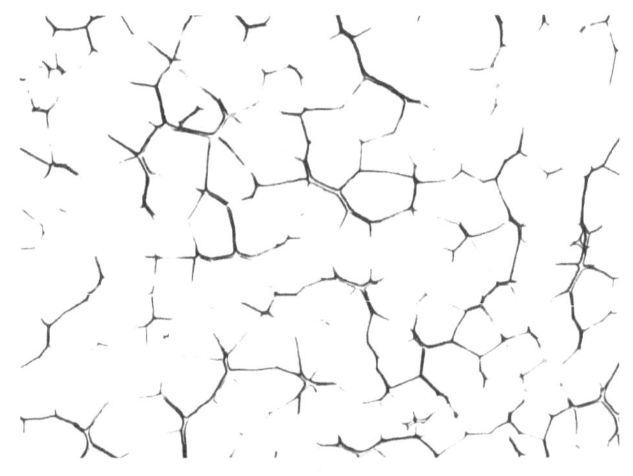

CHAPTER EIGHT

Fractured Foundations

Things had always fallen apart, one way or another. It had become a pattern I couldn't ignore, no matter how much I wished it would be different this time. And after the breakup, when it felt like everything had been torn to pieces, I kept thinking–maybe, maybe this time, it wouldn't happen. Maybe there was something I hadn't seen yet, a moment I hadn't reached.

But I always got there, to that point where one had to accept the inevitable. It was like a rhythm of my life, a constant cycle of hope, disappointment, the slow, crushing return to reality.

But then there came the idea of a new house, a new beginning. And god, how much I wanted that. For a while, it felt like I could actually build something, something that wouldn't fall apart. It wasn't just about the house—it was the sense of control, of having a say in my future, in my life.

For once, maybe I could get something right. Maybe this time, the walls would be strong enough to keep everything out. Maybe this time, everything would finally be different.

It was a strange kind of excitement that I felt on the day we moved into the new house. It was not like the other houses we had lived in; those were just stops along the way, temporary resting places for the chaos that was our life. But this one? This one was different.

The house was still a shell with no real definition yet, but I could already feel its potential. I could already picture what it could be. It was like the empty space had a promise to it. It wasn't grand or perfect, but it was ours.

I remember stepping over the threshold for the first time. It was cold inside, the kind of chill that made your breath visible in the air. No curtains, no furniture-not even a single rug on the floor. Just bare walls and the remnants of what the old house had once been: a dusty skeleton of a place being torn down to make room for something new.

But I loved it. I stood there for a moment, just taking it in, letting the quiet fill me. For the first time in years, I didn't feel like an outsider. I wasn't just living in someone else's space, hoping to make myself small enough not to be noticed. This was mine. Or at least, it was supposed to be.

The house itself was nothing special. Raw walls, unfinished ceilings, and floors echoing empty. Like it hadn't made up its mind about being a house yet, that didn't matter to me. It was blank paper. The kind I have always wanted but never really got. My mind was working fast as all the rooms began taking form in my head. The kitchen would be there, and the living room would be here.

My bedroom would face the street with enough light coming in through the window to make everything seem real. I imagined sitting by that window, just watching the world go by, feeling as if I had finally found a place to belong.

Everything had been temporary for so long. We had lived with my Nanu and Nani for what felt like forever, and I had always told myself that I would leave one day. But now that we were finally here, in this house that we were building from scratch, I could see it all unfolding in front of me—a new beginning.

A fresh start.

This is why, whenever I could help it, I kept telling myself that this house was a new version of me, a place where I could escape the weight of the past, a place where I could finally be something more than what I had always been.

It was my mother who worked hard to get us to where we were. I knew how much work she had put into this house, how many nights she spent working, making sure everything was in order. She was proud of it, and I could see why.

It wasn't just about the bricks and mortar—it was about creating something from nothing, about carving out a piece of the world that was just ours. She had wanted this so badly, and now we were here, standing on the threshold of something that felt like it could finally be real.

I loved it here. The quiet felt different. The house felt different. I would spend hours walking through the empty rooms, imagining what they would look like once everything was finished. There was something about the silence that made me feel as though I could finally breathe. The space was wide open, and for the first time in my life, I didn't feel crowded by the weight of everything that had come before.

It was just me and the house, and maybe that was enough. I could already hear the laughter that might fill the rooms, the sound of my mom's voice echoing through the hallways, and the distant hum of life outside. I could already see myself here, living in this place that was mine, a place where the ghosts of the past might finally be quiet.

But as the days went on and the house slowly took shape, the excitement began to fade. The walls that had promised so much now felt cold. The rooms that had felt so wide open began to feel too small. The house, like everything else in my life, wasn't as simple as I had thought. It wasn't just a house; it was a symbol of everything I had been running from. Cracks started to appear, not in the walls but in the spaces between us. It wasn't the house that was the problem; it was the things we had left behind, the things we hadn't addressed.

My dad wasn't part of this new beginning. He had broken into the picture a couple of times before, but now that the house was taking form, it was evident that he wasn't going to be included in this new life.

His presence lingered in the air, like a shadow that hadn't fully dissipated, and I felt the tension build every time he wasn't around. It wasn't long before the cracks in our little family began to show again, and the weight of everything that had been left unsaid began to weigh on me in ways I didn't know how to handle.

For a time, I had convinced myself that this house was my way out, my sanctuary from everything else. But the more I tried to convince myself of that, the more I realised that it wasn't just the house that was broken-it was me.

I wanted to love this place, wanted to hold on to that idea of it, and that it was something which could fix everything. Of course, it was not the way it ever worked: the house wasn't going to make anything better. I wasn't going to turn into another person just because I was somewhere else. The ghosts in my past were not disappearing. They slid in unobtrusively like dust through the cracks. They lurked out of reach, just over there and out of sight.

And in the quiet of the house, I began to listen more clearly than ever to them. It didn't take very long for the house to change. What I thought would be the start of a fresh future, a place where maybe, just maybe, the rest of the world could slow down a little, transformed quickly into another stage of chaos.

My father came back, but he was not coming back; my father stormed back into our lives, loud and impossible to ignore. He wasn't supposed to stay. Of course, that much was clear from the beginning, but when had he ever cared about the supposed rules?

He walked in with the kind of authority that seemed to make it seem as though we had all been waiting for him. His presence stretched across the house like a dark shadow, spilling into every corner, leaving no space untouched.

I was fourteen, barely more than a shadow myself, and the look of him filled me with the same dread I'd learned to live with years before. I stayed hidden as much as possible. I hid in hallways and shrank into silence whenever he was nearby. It didn't matter.

The first fight began over something small, something insignificant enough to forget. That's how it always went, though: him turning the smallest things into weapons. His voice filled the room, drowning out every other sound, cutting through whatever thin sense of peace we had managed to build in this house.

My mother fought back, but not in a way that felt like she cared about winning—more like she cared about being loud enough to make him shut up. Their argument wasn't fought; it was just noise, getting louder and uglier until it felt like the walls were going to crack under the weight of it.

It wasn't long before the shouting turned towards me. His eyes would find me quiet in my corner, and something about my stillness made him angrier. He'd start with words, sharp and deliberate, poking at every vulnerability he could find. I tried not to react. I thought maybe if I didn't give him anything, he'd lose interest. But I was wrong.

With a quick motion, he pushed me back, using one hand to send me tumbling awkwardly off-balance and into the solid door frame that stood behind me. Not so much the physical agony of the fall hurt me but the weight of his scorn, multiplied by the sound of his laugh, full of disdain that hung in the air. "Look at you," he spat out venomously, narrowing his eyes as if he believed he could peel away my outer skin and reveal nothing of worth underneath it. "Pathetic."

I wouldn't let myself cry, definitely not then. Crying was a luxury I simply could not indulge in, especially not with him watching me. So I clasped my fists shut firmly, feeling my nails pierce deep into the fleshy softness of my palms, so sharply it felt like they might well crack through the skin, and remained silent.

My mother was there, her arms crossed, standing a few feet away. Her face set in that unreadable expression she had perfected–part judgment, part indifference. She said nothing to stop him, nothing to intervene. And when he stormed out, she remained silent, her silence much louder than anything he could have said.

Later, when the house was quiet, and I thought maybe she would come to me with some comfort, she turned instead with words that struck harder than his hands ever could. "You didn't even try," she said, her voice so calm it felt like ice. "You just stood there like a coward.".

I opened my mouth, ready to say something-anything-to defend myself at that moment, to remind her firmly that I was only fourteen years old and that he was, in fact, a monster twice the size of me, which made the situation all the more unfair. However, to my dismay, no words came out at all. Her intense stare seemed to cut through me like a sharp knife, dissecting every single inch of my being and leaving me feeling utterly exposed and vulnerable. As I stood there, I became convinced that I was as worthless as she had made me feel throughout our confrontation.

"That's why he doesn't respect you. That's why you'll never be anything," she added, and then she left me there, alone with her words.

For weeks after, every glance at my reflection brought her voice back to me. Coward. Weak. Nothing. Those words echoed relentlessly, a cruel loop in my head, taunting me with every look. So, I started going to the gym—not because I thought it would truly fix anything, but because it felt like something I had to do. Like somehow, sweating it out could silence those voices.

Her voice became the rhythm of every lift, every push, every rep. The movement felt like dragging not just the weight of the equipment but the expectations and judgments she had chained to me. It wasn't just about proving something to her or anyone else. It became about proving to myself—that I wasn't as worthless as her words made me feel.

But the mirror had another truth to tell. No matter how much I strained, how much I built up my body, the real scars weren't visible. They were buried too deep, etched into a place that no amount of strength could shield. A part of me knew the effort was futile, but it was all I had left to hold onto. The house, once a warm and cosy place that felt like a real home, was no longer this to me. It became instead a huge stage, and I felt doomed to fail in every single act I tried to perform there. My father, instead of leaving us behind, chose to stay but sank deeper into the very spaces that were meant to be ours, places that used to resound with joy and love.

His voice, with frustration and discontent, echoed ominously through the walls, and his anger seemed to pour over into every single room, making them treacherous minefields where I had to tread carefully. My mother, instead of providing me with the protection and solace I needed, just joined him in this whirlwind of negativity; her disappointment pierced through me sharper and more painful than any blade ever could.

And when the night-time did come, when the house was silent and motionless, letting the shadows stretch and stretch in every direction, I found myself sitting alone in the darkling enveloping shroud, where I recited their words over and over and over again... Weak. Useless. Failure. And those painful echoes would not be still or fade.

It wasn't just the physical push, nor the yelling that had broken out in anger, or even the hurtful words my father hurled my way that managed to haunt the quiet, shadowy corners of my mind long after the incident had come and gone. I could have survived and carried all of that emotional baggage with me –just barely, but I could have managed to do so. What really broke me, left me feeling utterly shattered, was the sound of her voice. It wasn't raised in a heated manner, nor was it trembling with uncontrollable rage; instead, it was calm and cold, as if she'd thought through every word that came out of her mouth and made a deliberate decision that those particular words were meant to hurt.

"You really didn't try at all." When she said those words, it felt like the air around my being had imploded in a way that felt as though every molecule in the room had decided to unite against me at once. What struck me was not so much the content of her words but the tone in which she said them—the sound itself was more impactful than the phrasing.

It was the way her voice slid under my skin and dug its way into my psyche in a way that my father's violent outbursts never could. My father's aggression was always predictable; his anger was both blunt and uncreative, without any nuance or complexity. This? This was something altogether different and much more unnerving.

This was a deep betrayal, which was cleverly veiled within a mask of reason, well designed to strike at a point I never thought she would.

For a good long period, she was the only obstacle that stood between me and him, steadfast in her resistance. In reflecting on those afternoons at my grandparents, I realise she was the bulwark he could not penetrate: the reason why his suffocating rage had to stop at the very doorjamb of a room, unable to press forward any further. Again, not a hero; certainly not that. Yet she was enough for her purpose, at least that's what I thought back then.

That illusion came crashing down in an instant the moment she turned her gaze upon me, a gaze that was both cold and cutting. It wasn't just that she didn't save me this time around it was much deeper; she became part of the very attack itself.

You're showing signs of vulnerability," she said one other time, on the day when I gained the courage to ask her why she hadn't acted lately to intervene in this mess. "You let him walk all over your emotions and your lines in the sand. What kind of man lets that happen?

I felt an overwhelming urge to scream out loud that I was only fourteen years old. I was at the edge of my emotional capacity, barely managing to hold on amidst the turmoil. But even though I had put forth every possible effort and done absolutely everything within my power, it still seemed to never be sufficient to meet expectations.

And her harsh words didn't allow any space for that. They completely erased the essence of the child that I still was deep inside and depicted me as something fundamentally broken, something inherently unworthy of love and acceptance.

The worst part was that I believed her.

She had always had such a fine sense of just where to bring the most painful emotional hurts. Maybe this is part of what narcissistic mothers have—a special talent to turn the very people most caring for them into the personal scapegoats on whom their frustrations and other insecurities fall.

Her words were never like my father's: loud and precipitous. Instead, calculated and slow-burning in their impact, they entered the mind with a hurt that would not easily be forgotten but lingered long after she had vacated the room, leaving echoes of pain.

And it was only after that special moment that I started to view her in a way so unmistakably different from what had gone before, but this transformation did not come overnight; rather, it came piecemeal, in tiny fragments, like a confusing puzzle I had no great interest in solving. I recall moments when I would suddenly catch myself looking at how she would smile at the words of someone complimenting her for enduring such a beast of a husband so well.

In those instances, her eyes would flash with an intensity that indicated she loved every minute of being treated to the praise and admiration coming her way. She portrayed the victim so masterfully and convincingly that even I, for many years, found myself drawn to her portrayal and completely bought into her story.

But then, when we moved into our new house, all the frontage she had kept up for all these years started to wear down. She no longer needed me to shelter her or rescue her; I had merely become an added aspect to her complicated game, merely another toy that she could discard at will. What happened to all those times that I became inconvenient? Well then, she made me something disposable, easily cast off without giving it another second thought. Her words didn't just hurt me emotionally; they completely changed my sense of self. They made me question every moment when I thought she cared for me, every time she called me her "good boy" when I helped her with the dishes or stood up for her when my father criticised her.

Was that love? Or was it just convenient for her? And so, at this very present hour, I just can't be definitive about anything, or at least, I find out about one thing- that the individual I always thought her to be disappeared the moment she laid all the blame for his mistreatment of her on my shoulders. What was one person who had seemed the only person left that could be there, available to depend on in one's most desperate hours, had become the very adversary at my shoulder. As I settled down to sleep in the quiet of my room, lying in bed at night and gazing up at the various cracks that marred the ceiling above me, his words resounded in my mind with a clarity and an intensity far greater than his shouts had ever achieved at their loudest.

The scars didn't show, but they were there—etched into the way I thought, the way I breathed, the way I approached people who tried to care. Trust became a foreign concept, like a language I'd once spoken fluently but had now forgotten.

It wasn't so much about her betrayal; it was just that it came from somebody I thought was a sanctuary; it was learning that that one person who had to save me, the one who had to shield me, was the one person who ended up cutting the deepest part of me.

Every subsequent interaction felt like a test I couldn't pass. I questioned everything: every smile, every kind word, every hand extended in friendship. Was it real, or was there a blade waiting to be unsheathed, hidden behind it, and just waiting for the moment when I let my guard down? I didn't know, and I couldn't afford to find out.

So, I didn't. I built walls instead, higher and thicker with every passing year. I became good at deflecting, at keeping people at a distance where they couldn't reach the parts of me that still bled. It was safer this way. No one could hurt me if I never gave them the chance.

But safety came at a price. The isolation I had chosen for myself was stifling and heavy, like trying to breathe underwater. I wanted to trust, to believe in someone the way I had once believed in her. But the fear of being wrong again was stronger than the hope of being right.

Even now, I catch myself doubting people who have done nothing to deserve it. A kind gesture feels suspicious; a compliment feels rehearsed. I do not let them in, not really, because a voice in the back of my mind whispers that it's only a matter of time before they turn their kindness into cruelty.

And maybe that's the real legacy of what happened in that house—not just the bruises or the harsh words, but the way it broke something inside me that I'm not sure can ever be fixed.

CHAPTER NINE

Broken Mirrors

Trust is one of the weirdest things. Years in the building and seconds to break. You are always being told it's the essence, the base of every significant relationship. You never hear how it's that the very same people you entrust with the most will be the same ones that shatter your foundation.

They do not warn you of how sometimes this betrayal isn't loud, not obvious at all; sometimes it is a whisper. A moment. A silent act that leaves you questioning everything you've ever known about love, loyalty, and safety.

And the worst part? It's the people closest to you who do it best.

I used to think my mother was different. She was the exception to this unspoken rule of heartbreak; she wasn't perfect—no one is—but she was mine. When the world outside seemed hostile and cruel, she was the one who made it feel manageable. I built my understanding of safety around her. Around the way, she'd hold my hand when things got tough. Around the way, she'd sit beside me when the walls of our old house echoed with arguments I didn't want to hear.

It wasn't just love; it was dependency. The kind you do not even realise you have till it is torn from your very being.

So, leaving the grandparents' house filled my heart with a weird sense of hope. It was no life we had dreamt of, but it was something. A new start. Our start. The new house was not perfect; it smelled of dust and wet concrete, and the paint was uneven, but it belonged to us. I remember walking through empty rooms, running fingers over cool walls as though, in some versions of our lives, it was bound to settle.

I was 14, just a skinny kid with more hope than sense. I wanted to believe that the house would change things. That my mom and I could finally have the life we talked about in whispers late at night, back when I still trusted her without question.

And for a while, it almost felt real. We unpacked boxes and laughed about where to put the furniture. My mom smiled more, her tired eyes softening in a way I hadn't seen in years. The chaos felt distant like we'd left it behind with the old house. I started thinking that maybe, just maybe, life could be different.

But that's the thing about hope.

It blinds you.

The new house, its coloured walls and a fresh coat of paint did not only smell like new plaster; it also smelled like a possibility yet to come. For weeks, I clung to that thin hope like a lifeline thrown to me in the turbulent waters, sure in every fibre of my being that we had finally escaped the relentless chaos that marked our previous life.

Houses, however, do not have the power to change people. Solid walls, no matter how new, cannot stop the relentless tide of memories that cling to us. And sometimes, the cracks in a foundation can run far too deep to ever be fixed or mended.

It started slow. A shouted word here, a slammed door there.

I have always believed that there is an unwritten law that connects parents to their children, a kind of sacred contract that one should not violate. No matter how desperate things may get or how fractured the family may seem, there will always be at least one person in that family with whom you can trust your life.

This would be someone who would never betray your trust or leave you hanging during your hour of need, someone who, under no circumstances, would turn you over to the pack.

My mother was the one who had, of course, taken on that position in my life. Or so I had assumed, at any rate.

I cannot really decide if it was the words she used or the specific tone in which she expressed them, but something within me cracked irreparably on that day. It was not just that she had laid the blame squarely at my doorstep; she turned the entire story around.

To her, I wasn't the victim of circumstances anymore; I had become the symbol of failure itself. I had now become the weakling. I was now the bottom-line reason why everything around us was crumbling and falling apart.

It is really very difficult to relate the intense emotional hurt felt when one is betrayed by a person whom you gave all and built your life upon—who you built your sense of security and safety on. Initially, it was not anger, as people would assume when this happens. Instead, it was this total bewilderment that befell me.

The bewilderment was raw and overwhelming and even bordering on choking, which had the mind to start thinking in such ways that made me doubt everything I ever knew about myself: who I am at my core, what value I held in this world, and whether I ever would be enough for anybody or anything.

Her words could touch so deeply; she knew exactly where to go to bring it into the more fragile part of my being, which was already pretty delicate. You did not even erect a proper defence when this guy went after you, either. That is not surprisingly the way he has you.

I felt a compelling need to scream out loud to let her know how I had fought against all odds to be able to express how fiercely I had battled for it. I wanted to show that I had indeed done everything in my power to rectify things. But, however strong this urge was, words just would not leave my lips.

I stayed there, absolutely silent, under the heavy and oppressive weight of her disappointment like a suffocating blanket that made breathing quite impossible.

That night, I was lying in bed, staring blankly at the ceiling of my room as I replayed the same scene over and over in my mind. I was trying to analyse the moment so that I could figure out where I went wrong and exactly what I could have done to change the direction of things more favourably. But however many different scenarios I pictured playing out in my head, the result was the same every time: I just wasn't enough.

It was then that I started to feel an intense level of self-hatred. It was not like in the movies, with the loud, dramatic, and theatrical expression of emotions, but rather a subtle, sneaky kind of way that slowly ate away at my well-being. It felt like a deep-seated form of self-hatred that would creep into my thoughts and feelings at the most unsuspecting moments when I least expected it.

I began to see every one of my imperfections and every small weakness that I possessed. Whenever I caught a glimpse of myself in the mirror, a revolting feeling of distaste washed over me at what I was seeing staring back. My arms were thin and feeble. My cheeks were hollow and gaunt. I felt like a boy who could not even defend himself, not to mention be able to protect anyone else around him.

However, the most difficult part of my experience was not only how I felt about myself but it was all the overwhelming emotions that were upon me. It was as if I had an unseen weight attached to me, reminding me, day in and day out, that deep down, I believed I just wasn't good enough. No matter how hard I tried to throw it off and get rid of this feeling, it stayed attached to me like a shadow that would not let go.

I don't think my mom ever realised the impact of her words. Or maybe she did, and that's what made it worse. A part of me wanted to believe she lashed out because she was hurting too, that it wasn't personal. But another part of me couldn't shake the thought that she meant every word.

She had always been so good at the flaws. She could spin them around and make weapons out of them when she needed to. It hadn't been the first time, but it felt different this time. This time, it wasn't about a grade I hadn't scored high enough on or the way that I was carrying myself in public. This time, it was about who I was on the inside.

WEAK

That word played nonstop in my mind as it etched itself on my identity. I almost began to believe it, especially when I knew it couldn't be. But from the mouth of someone you trust, who you base your world around, this word stops being just any word. It becomes an unshakeable truth.

I tried to tap into it to disprove her. I later in life signed up for the gym, thinking if I could get my body more toned, then maybe the rest of me would be more like that, too. But no matter how many hours I spent pumping iron or running on that stupid treadmill, I couldn't run from that feeling.

I was doing it for the way I looked at myself when standing in front of the mirror every day. No matter how much I felt I progressed, nothing I ever did could be enough. I was always showing some trace of strength but seeing the ghost, the shadow, of the man who used to be me. The weak, ineffective, skinny boy who could not stand up to his dad. The boy his mom blamed and pointed her fingers at whatever went wrong.

Obsession over the gym. Not to be fit but to punish myself. Every rep, every set, every droplet of sweat was my atonement for failure. I wasn't merely getting stronger; I was piecing myself back together.

But no matter how hard I tried, I just couldn't shake the feeling that I was fighting a losing battle. It wasn't so much what my mom had said to me; it was the way she looked at me like I was a disappointment.

Like I wasn't worth saving.

It's funny how love can feel like a noose. Someone can claim to care for you while slowly tightening the grip, leaving just enough room for you to breathe but not enough to live. That was what it was like with her. Her love wasn't unconditional; it came with strings attached–long, invisible ones that tugged at my every move, every decision, every word.

She had a way to turn everything around herself. My successes? Reflection of what she did for me. My failures? As proof that I was worthless in front of everything that she had done for me. It was not merely in what she said; it was the way she said them. That little tilted head, those disappointed sighs, unspoken words louder than what even a shout could be.

I recall one instance when I attempted to stand up for myself, just once, thinking that it might do the trick. I was fourteen and full of that misplaced teenage confidence that fades as quickly as it comes. I told her that I needed space and that her constant criticism was suffocating me. She laughed, not the kind of laugh that softens a moment, but the kind that cuts through you like a blade.

"Space?" she said, her voice dripping with mockery. "You think you've earned the right to ask for that? After everything I've done for you?"

And just like that, I was back in my place. Small. Silent. Grateful.

Her words weren't just words; they were weapons. She didn't yell; she didn't have to. One sentence from her could take all my confidence, all my sense of self, and my will to fight back. "You'll never be enough," she'd say, sometimes without saying it at all. It was in the way she looked at me, the way she measured me against some impossible standard that I didn't even know existed.

She'd play the victim so well, twisting every situation to make it seem like I was the one who hurt her. If I tried to explain how her words made me feel, she'd turn it around, reminding me of all the times I'd let her down. "After all I've done for you, this is how you repay me?" she'd ask, and suddenly, I'd be the one apologising.

But the worst part wasn't her words—it was how much I believed them. How deeply they rooted themselves in me, growing like weeds in the cracks of my self-esteem. She made me question everything about myself: my worth, my abilities, my right to take up space.

Even the moments that should have had everything to do with me were always about her. When I got good grades, it was because she pushed me. When I failed, it was because I hadn't listened enough to her. She converted every triumph into a testament to her greatness and every failure into a reminder of mine.

But the thing about her narcissism is that it wasn't all bad. There were moments–fleeting, rare moments–when she'd wrap her arms around me and tell me she was proud. And I'd cling to those moments like a lifeline, convincing myself that maybe, just maybe, I was enough for her.

But those moments never lasted. They were always followed by the inevitable crash, the reminder that her love came at a cost, and it was a price I'd never be able to pay.

After all that, how could I trust anybody? How could I believe that love was not a transaction, that it was not just another debt to be paid off? She taught me that love is not a safe place but a battlefield. It was her battlefield. Every time I tried to go out of line, she reminded me that no matter how much I gave, it would never be enough.

I stopped trusting people after her. I stopped believing that anyone could love me without an agenda. It's hard to trust when your own mother–the one person you think should have your back, the one person who's supposed to love you unconditionally–turns every good moment into a tool for her ego. How can you open up to any soul when that one being who should know you best only ever looked into you as a mirror of her own reflection?

I spent years trying to figure out where I went wrong, trying to fix myself, trying to make myself enough for someone who would never be satisfied. It didn't matter what I did; the goalposts kept moving. Each time I thought I'd reached the target, it shifted just out of reach. And no matter how hard I worked, no matter how much I gave, the satisfaction was always fleeting.

That's when the perfectionism started. Not because I wanted to be perfect but because I couldn't handle the idea of failing again. I couldn't live with the thought of letting someone down the way I let her down. Every time I did something wrong, every time I didn't meet some invisible standard I didn't even know existed—I was flooded with that same feeling of inadequacy that she'd planted in me.

Perfectionism became my shield. If I could do everything perfectly, maybe I could avoid the pain. Maybe I could avoid the feeling of being unwanted, unloved, and not enough. If I could be perfect, I could stop the world from tearing me apart. But the problem with perfection is that it's a lie—a lie that's impossible to live up to.

The irony? The more I tried to be perfect, the worse it got. Because perfection isn't just unattainable–it's suffocating. And that suffocating feeling, that fear of failure, it just made me more isolated. It made me pull away from people. It made me question everything I did.

I started to hate myself even more than I had before. I hated how I never was good enough. I hated how I always had to be something I wasn't just to get a little bit of love. I hated the way I was pushing myself to be perfect, knowing deep down that it was never going to be enough.

And that is when issues started with trust. They did not simply grow overnight. It was brought along by years of conditioning– without words–told over and over that I would not be enough. I'd never do enough no matter what I did.

I couldn't trust people with my heart. I couldn't trust them with my time, my energy, my everything. The thought of being vulnerable terrified me. I couldn't open up to anyone because I was terrified they'd see me the way she saw me–flawed, unworthy, and incapable of being loved.

The truth is that I became my own worst enemy. I internalised everything. Her criticisms, her neglect, her indifference-them all became my inner voice, telling me that I wasn't good enough, that I could never be enough.

And so I kept building walls, walls between me and the world, walls between me and the people who cared about me, walls so high I didn't even know how to climb over them any more.

I couldn't trust anyone–I couldn't trust anyone–because how could I? How could I trust the world, I ask you when the one person I thought I should be able to depend on had turned all my thinking about love over.

After four long years.

For a while, I indulged in the illusion of maybe, just maybe, someone could offer the kind of love I had been seeking all my life–something real, something that would mend the cracks in me.

I fell into the comfort of her presence, thinking that this was to be the answer; she was one person who could rewrite the story I had been telling myself for years. She was not a stranger in my mind but a vision I built from everything I wanted to believe.

I was searching for someone who could provide me with the acceptance that I had been longing for, someone who could fill the void that I couldn't fill myself.

But no sooner had that hope blossomed than withered just as violently as it had. For there was the love I most desperately craved, which I thought might penetrate enough to break through walls: yet to my surprise, I could see it was merely a repetition of my own misplaced faith-what I thought genuine but fell apart in front of my eyes, unravelling like a seam. The further I tried, the stronger the distance between us began to feel.

I had hoped for something different, but in the end, I was left with nothing more than the echo of my own unmet expectations. What had felt like a promise quickly became just another broken dream, and the pattern I had tried so hard to escape–of giving too much, trusting too easily–played itself out again.

I was left hollow, wondering if I had ever known what real love felt like or if I had been chasing shadows all along.

In the end, the reality was clear: no one could fix me. Not her, not anyone. I had been searching for someone to show me the way, but in the silence that followed, I realised that the path to healing was something only I could walk.

And there it was–the truth that hit harder than anything else. The one thing I refused to admit was that I was the one who let myself believe. I built it all up, piece by fool, convinced the walls would hold. But they didn't. And they never would.

I was weak. And the worst part? I kept choosing it. Over and over, I kept reaching for something that never was. Because at some point, you stop trying to fix things and start wanting to believe they can be fixed. But I was not a fixing kind of boy in this life, not this time, not ever, and that's something I do know.

I cannot afford to love again. Not like that. Not with the same blind faith, the same open heart that always ends up shattered on the ground, waiting for someone to pick it up. But they never do. No one does. And deep down, I know I've known this all along, even if I refused to face it.

So, no more. No more hope. No more trust. No more pretending I could be someone else, someone better. I have been all right about being lonely. It is safer in this way. The fewer things you expect, the lesser the hurt. I've learned that lesson rather well, too.

I will never be enough. I'll never be the person I wanted to be. And maybe that's the only truth I'll ever truly know. So, here's the promise I make to myself: I will never let anyone in again. Not like that. Not in a way that would make me feel anything. Because feelings are dangerous, and I've seen what they can do. I've seen how they can destroy everything.

I'm done with this. I'm done with trying because trying only makes you look like a fool in the end.

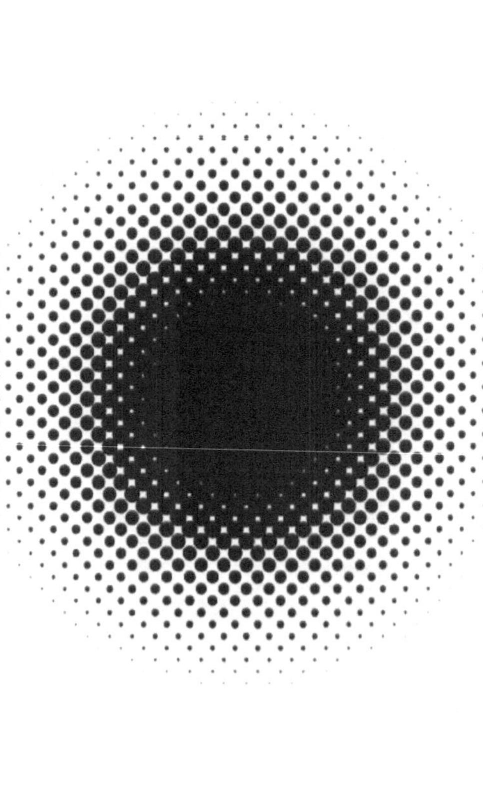

CHAPTER TEN

Echoes of the Past

A heaviness hangs in the air, one you can't quite name but feel in every breath–like dragging a weight you've grown so accustomed to, you've forgotten what it feels like to walk free. It doesn't come all at once; it creeps in, taking over inch by inch, moment by moment, until it's everywhere. This is what depression feels like. This is what anxiety claws at.

There are days when the sun feels too bright, too intrusive, and you wish for clouds, for darkness–anything to match the storm inside. People around you laugh and talk, moving through life as if it's simple. And maybe it is for them. But for you? Every small decision feels like a monumental task. Every interaction feels like you're walking a tightrope, balancing between the need to connect and the fear of falling.

You tell yourself you're just tired. Maybe it's nothing. It may pass. But deep down, you know better. You've been here before, haven't you? This suffocating fog that presses against your chest, the way your mind spirals into a labyrinth of thoughts that have no escape, the fear of being alone, and yet the overwhelming relief of not having to pretend around anyone.

It's in the way your heart races when your phone vibrates, the dread that someone might need something from you—a conversation, a favour, a response you're not ready to give. It's in the way you replay interactions in your mind, dissecting every word, every pause, convincing yourself you've said something wrong. And then comes the silence. The kind that's deafening, where your mind whispers all the ways you're not enough.

But it is not the whispers. It is the echoes. The voices from the past, the memories that you have buried but cannot help but take with you, rise up when you least expect them to, dragging you back into moments you may want to forget. Worst of all, you believe them now. The critical words that others have said to you have become your own reality. The rejection that is carved into your identity. The errors that play on repeat, convincing you this is all you'll ever be.

It's a paradox, is it not? To seek connection yet fear vulnerability. To want to be seen yet not really known. Because if they knew really knew, they'd run, wouldn't they? Or worse, they'd stay just to remind you of everything that you are not. So keep them at arm's length by smiling just enough to make it look okay and then offering just enough to prevent those questions from being asked.

And then there are days when it's not enough. The weight becomes too much, and you break. The panic sets in sharp and swift, stealing your breath and making your heart pound to get out.

You try to find a grounding and breathe, but it's like drowning, like screaming underwater where no one can hear you. You've told yourself that it is just a phase. That you'll grow out of it. But as the years pass, it becomes harder to believe.

Maybe you have tried to explain it to someone. Maybe you have even opened up, let them see the cracks. But their responses? A mix of pity and discomfort, as if your pain is something they'd rather not touch. They say things like, "Just think positive," or "You're stronger than this," as if the solution is that simple. And you nod, forcing a smile because explaining it would take more energy than you have.

This leads to you wondering whether this is what you're supposed to be like you'll never know your former person. Now replaced by that hollow imitation, living but never truly understanding it's even happening because you can survive, although you learn the art of seeming just fine while going quietly about disintegrating. But at the back of this mind, there lies a tiny part refusing to throw in the towel and move on with life. That stubborn little flicker of hope perhaps that things are going to go better.

Depression isn't just sadness. It is when joy isn't there, an inability to feel when everything around you says otherwise. It is the feeling that replaces pain: numbness; a feeling that overtakes a person when caring becomes too much: apathy. And anxiety? It is the constant humming of fear, the waiting for disaster, even though everything is all right. Altogether, they create this storm that's exhausting yet impossible to escape from.

But here's the thing: you are not alone. Even when it feels like you are, even when the world feels miles away and indifferent, others have walked this way before you and survived it. And though that doesn't make the burden any lighter, it reminds you that it's possible. Maybe, just maybe, the echoes don't have to define you. Maybe the story doesn't have to end here.

For now, though, it's okay to feel. To sit with the pain and acknowledge it for what it is. Because pretending it's not there won't make it go away. And while the road ahead might be long and uncertain, the fact that you're still here, still fighting, is proof that you're stronger than you think.

And that? That's where this chapter begins.

Days began to blend together. Time lost all significance as my thoughts weighed me down. Quiet reflection turned into persistent whispers; it was the voices that spoke to every failure, every mistake, every time I was not enough. But these weren't just my thoughts – they were shadows of things said, promises broken, and trust shattered. My mother's words had somehow woven themselves into the fabric of my being, and I couldn't seem to unravel them no matter how hard I tried.

I used to think that if I tried hard enough if I became good enough, she'd see me. Really see me. But now? Now, I wasn't sure if I even wanted her to. The protector, the one who shielded me from the storms, felt like a cruel lie, a story I told myself to survive. And with every cruel remark, every dismissive glance, it became clearer that the person I'd relied on wasn't who I thought she was.

Her narcissism wasn't out there, not the kind that you read about in books or see dramatised in films. No, it was subtle, insidious, a quiet erosion of the self. It was in the way she'd praise me one moment only to tear me down the next. The way her affection felt conditional, fleeting, like a prize I could never quite earn.

It was in the way she'd twist the narrative, making herself the victim in every situation, leaving me to question my reality. And worst of all, it was in the way she'd weaponise my vulnerabilities, using the very things I'd confided in her as ammunition.

I remember one evening vividly. The air was thick with the scent of damp earth after a rainstorm, and the house felt colder than usual. I had mustered the courage to share something with her, a dream I had held so tightly in my hands, afraid it might break under the weight of scrutiny.

Instead of support, I was met with laughter. Not the warm, encouraging kind, but the cruel, cutting kind that left wounds invisible to the eye but impossible to ignore.

"You? Doing that?" she'd said, her voice dripping with scepticism. "Don't be ridiculous."

Her words hurt me far more than any punch ever could. They didn't just hurt; they took the stuffing out of me, leaving hollow a place for what I thought I was. I wanted to scream, to argue, to make her see the harm she'd done. But I stayed silent, words there in my throat like bits of glass. Because deep inside me, a part believed her. Thought I was never good enough, never would be.

And so, I turned inward. If I couldn't trust her, the only person I thought would have my back, then who could I trust? The answer was no one. Not even myself. And so, I became hyper-aware of every action, every word, scrutinising them with a lens of self-doubt. Perfection became my shield, my way to protect myself from further disappointment. If I could just be perfect, maybe I'd be worthy. Maybe I'd finally be enough.

But perfection is a cruel master. It asks for everything and gives nothing back. And no matter how much I tried, it remained always just out of sight. The cracks in my façade grew wider, and the pressure built until it became unbearable. But I couldn't stop. To stop would be to face the truth: no amount of achievement, no level of perfection, could possibly fill the void left by her betrayal.

Even now, at eighteen, the scars remain. They've shaped me in ways I'm only beginning to understand. The anxiety that grips me in social situations, the depression that lingers like a shadow, the trust issues that make every relationship feel like walking a tightrope, they all trace back to those moments. To her.

And then there's the self-hatred. The quiet loathing that creeps in during the dead of night, whispering all the ways I've failed, all the reasons I'll never be enough. It's a voice that's become all too familiar, one that I've fought to silence but can't seem to escape. It tells me that I'm broken, unworthy, a product of my past with no hope for the future.

I would like to say that I have found a way to quiet that voice, to prove it wrong. But the truth is, it's a battle I'm still fighting. Some days, I win. On other days, it feels like the voice has already won before I've even opened my eyes. But through it all, there's a small, stubborn part of me that refuses to give up. That part clings to the hope that maybe, just maybe, I can find a way to heal. I can rewrite my story and become more than the sum of my scars.

For now, though, I'll keep writing. Because in these words, I find a sense of control, a way to make sense of the chaos. And maybe, just maybe, someone reading this will see themselves in these pages and feel a little less alone. Because if there's one thing I've learned, it's that pain, as isolating as it feels, is a universal experience. And sometimes, just knowing you're not alone can make all the difference.

The effects of my mother's words linger on much longer than I ever could have imagined. It wasn't just the damage of one single night, the laughter that hollowed me out, or the scepticism that cut deeper than any knife.

It was repetition, an unrelenting pattern of doubt cast over every achievement, every hope, every sliver of joy. Her voice was my inner monologue, a script I couldn't rewrite no matter how many times I tried.

Some days, I wonder if she even knew what the effect of her behaviour was, the ripple effect of her narcissistic tendencies. But most days, I don't think it matters. Intent doesn't erase the consequences, and her behaviour left scars I carry like invisible weights. They're not seen, not acknowledged by anyone but me, yet they dictate my every move, every decision.

I am eighteen years old today because of those scars. It's that craving for perfection, my inability to trust someone so much because I thought a parent would not harm me. The problem of vulnerability all sprouted during that period when my deepest wound was a result of one whom I believed should care and defend me, yet gave me the greatest pain instead.

And so I wrote, feeling this swirl of anger and sadness but this glimmer of hope inside as I finished this paragraph. Hope that, maybe through these words, I will find a way to let go. To heal.

Recovery is not a neat, straight line. Messy, painful, sometimes all those things against the person I've become. To disarm my pain was, at times, a kick in the gut regarding the identity I fashioned around it. That is scary. Who am I without my scars? The narrative clung to for so long?

And that is why sometimes I'm an asshole-not trying to undo the past but in complete revolt against it. I paint my nails black and blue, knowing it may cause people to stop and stare because, to them, I don't "fit." I hear whispers like Why would a straight dude do that? But honestly, it is not about them; it's about me.

It's about seeing the colour splash across my fingers like I'm taking control of the person I am, piece by piece. Some days, it feels like I'm screaming at my reflection, daring the world to judge me for things I never dared to judge myself for before. And some days, I don't know if I'm screaming at the world or at the version of me that lets it all happen.

These moments, the ones where I do something that feels so uncharacteristic, are the ones that breathe life back into me when the weight feels too much. They're sometimes stupid, maybe even reckless, but they're mine. Little acts of defiance against the narrative I never asked for.

And somehow, they keep me tethered to the present, reminding me that even if I haven't healed completely, I'm still alive enough to fight.

I don't have the answers. All I have is the hope that one day, I'll find them. And maybe, just maybe, these words will be the first step.

CHAPTER ELEVEN

The Edge of It All

The quiet was different this time. It should have felt like a relief after days of wrestling with the same thoughts–about who I was, what I carried, and all the shadows of my past. But it wasn't. It was the kind of silence that lingers after something breaks, a silence that holds weight, like the pause before a scream or a storm.

Maybe I thought I had finally learned how to exist in it. Perhaps, after everything, I could just let it sit beside me like an old familiar ghost.

But the truth is that silence does not always bring peace. Sometimes, it is merely a warning, a slow crawl before everything collapses. I didn't know that then.

I thought I was holding it all together. I could carry the weight alone, just like I had always done–pushed down every ugly thing until it sat deep enough to feel invisible. It worked, at least, for a while, or at least I convinced myself of that.

But the body remembers.

All that holding in screaming, swallowing anger, being cool–all those years were waiting to be paid back, like a forgotten debt. And the day they happened, my body simply decided to collect.

I didn't know what an anxiety attack felt like. I didn't even know something like that could happen to me. People talk about panic like it's just in your head like it's just fear you can snap out of. But when it happened for the first time, alone in that room, I didn't think it was anxiety–I thought I was dying.

It wasn't a bang. It came without a fight or any incident that marked a breaking point for my side. I was in my bed one sunny morning when I had considered it to be yet another day. Another day was spent lying that I was all okay. Another day passed, as going through routines that helped keep me human enough for others to believe I still survived.

But beneath it all, something had already shifted.

It started as just a feeling that seemed insignificant–something I could hardly describe, like that soft ripple on the face of a calm ocean at that moment when a furious tempest was about to be unleashed. There I sat, half asleep, hazy and confused by the aftermath of sleep, when suddenly I felt it:

constriction in my chest that made me sit up straight. At first, I believed it was because I was either sitting improperly or badly placed. So, I dismissed it; I shrugged it off while I tried to adjust myself in a way to ease the cramping feeling as one would when trying to get rid of the cramp. Yet no matter how I pushed it away, hard as I tried, I was unable to make that cramping feeling go.

I attempted to breathe deeply, as everyone is instructed to do whenever they are stressed or otherwise overwhelmed, but it didn't help. The air around me was heavy and dense like I wasn't getting enough into my lungs to fill it. It felt like my lungs were broken or out of whack.

My chest seemed to refuse any expansion, no matter how hard I tried to push a breath into my body. It was like I was being strangled, caught in distress, even though no one was physically touching me or causing that discomfort. My chest felt as if it was on fire due to the effort and as if something heavy was pushing on it, and nothing would stop it.

I stood up, somehow thinking that maybe getting my position changed might somehow ease me out of the situation. My knees sagged in almost a second. I felt as if they were useless and couldn't hold me up. The floor seemed to pitch under me; everything else around me was moving, like I was someplace in a strange, warped dream.

My heart was now pounding, beating with a constant thud that seemed impossible to ignore. It felt too big for my chest as if it were trying to break free from the confines of my ribcage and make a break for the open air. The sound of my heartbeat echoed through my skull, overwhelming all other sensations and drowning out everything else around me.

The walls that enclosed me seemed to feel closer, almost as if they were closing in, tightening around me with every beat. The air was thicker and heavier, making each breath a laborious task. My vision blurred–everything around me appeared to tilt and spin, creating a disorienting effect, as if I was losing my grip on reality itself, teetering on the edge of something far more unsettling.

I stretched out my arm, reaching for something to hang on to, to steady myself in this desperate lunge, reaching out for the bed's edge as if it were the only thing anchoring me in this world. My hands were shaking wildly; they were moving with a mind of their own, uncontrollable, without my will. When I looked down at them, a shiver went through me, and a dazed sense of confusion washed over me: what was going on, why were they shaking like that? I couldn't seem to stop the shakiness.

My palms were cold, and I could feel the moisture, the sweat, which wasn't helping the situation one bit. I tried to move forward two paces, but my legs bucked wildly, almost spasmodically, and could not bear my weight nor keep me standing on my feet. Heat flooded all through my body that seemed to scorch with the strength of some huge fire burning down through my veins, but then, almost in a twinkling, be matched by an icy, bone-shivering chill that set prickles up across my skin and made my flesh feel all gooseflesh. Sweat dripped down my back in heavy, wet rivulets which clung forlornly but that would not abate its throes. Indeed, it worsened the situation so that everything received depth and sharpness as never had come before.

Panic started clawing at me.

I was in a state in which I couldn't breathe at all, couldn't think clearly, couldn't make even the smallest movement, and I was paralysed, unable to do anything whatsoever. The room around me felt like it was slowly closing in on me, as if the very walls were squeezing me tighter and tighter, giving me an overwhelming feeling of being stuck and utterly trapped in a nightmarish scenario. My throat felt constricted as if it were narrowing with every single breath I attempted to take.

In a desperate attempt to call for help, I opened my mouth wide to scream, but nothing came out—just air escaping, thin and completely useless in that moment of dire need.

I gasped, but my lungs felt like they were shrinking as if the air wasn't meant for me. I could feel my body gradually shutting down as if it were running out of gas. My muscles, weak and shaking uncontrollably, were no longer responding to my will or my wishes.

My mind was screaming in desperation, but the words I wanted to say tragically found themselves lost and unable to find their way out. I reached out once more to grasp the edge of the bed firmly to try and hold myself up from falling completely onto the floor, but it felt as though my whole body was giving way beneath me as if I were fading out of reality piece by piece and losing my grip on everything around me.

And then it hit me. I don't know what clicked, but suddenly, it all made sense in a horrifying, undeniable way.

I'm dying.

The thought wasn't loud or dramatic but clear, as if it had always been there, just waiting to be realised. It wasn't a fear; it was a certainty. I wasn't ready, but it didn't matter. I was alone, and there was no one to help me. I found that I was not merely losing the ability to manage my body and its functions. Instead, I was also losing grip on my entire life and all the aspects that came with it.

I stepped back, again feeling my legs collapse beneath me, this time not quite holding my weight until the force of my back smacked into the wall of ice and unyielding material that supported it. The electric shock coursed all the way through me, earthed in a way that nothing else had ever come close to achieving. It was a moment of panic - to scream out, to shout out for anyone in earshot to come to me, please, but no words will come from my mouth.

I ended up on the floor, curled up like a child who wanted to hide in the world. My body shuddered violently, but I could not move. I could not fight it anymore. I just. Let go.

I wasn't aware of how much time elapsed in this world, either. Time did not feel present, either, even while everything out here continued to move about as it would in a functioning world.

It really felt like I was trapped in a whole different world and suspended in a time that would not pass. The air around me was still thick and dense but not as choking as it was before. Slowly, I realised that my breathing did not slow down completely but seemed shallow and hollow, still making me feel creepy in myself that I was not yet fully in this moment at all.

My chest hurt to breathe, but it was as if my lungs were holding back as if something was holding me from filling them all the way. I remained on the floor, shaking with the cold of the wall against my back.

The silence in the room was almost oppressive, deafening. It wasn't just quiet. It was almost as though the silence around me became something alive, something accusingly judgmental of me and judging me harshly for something. And it wasn't something tangible but a failure of unknown reason, something that somehow and somewhere in my own existence went wrong, so poorly or miserably that I'd barely know how to vocalise or even start mentioning the issue.

Walls everywhere saw everything happen, and now wait like one would be expecting to give the answer, some explanation of the mayhem happening before me, how could I explain the moment to the people? I wished to forget it all together. I wanted to just shove all of that inside and bury it under the weight of everything else that I was not prepared to face or deal with.

But I knew that I simply couldn't do that. It felt far too real and too raw just to dismiss. It lingered within me, relentlessly gnawing at the edges of my consciousness, waiting for the perfect moment to strike again. At that time, I was unaware of when it would happen again.

The aftermath felt worse than the actual event. I sat on the floor for hours, unable to move, afraid that it would return if I so much as shifted. My legs felt like dead weight, my arms limp at my sides. I stared at the sunlight crawling across the room, the golden beams mocking how ordinary the world looked as if nothing had just happened.

But something *had* happened. Something I didn't have a name for.

My body still felt foreign, like it wasn't entirely mine anymore. I could feel the faint tremors in my fingers, a lingering reminder that whatever had taken over me wasn't gone. It was hiding somewhere deep inside, waiting for its next chance.

When I finally gathered the courage to stand, my legs wobbled beneath me. I leaned against the wall, using it for support, as I dragged myself to the sink. My reflection caught me off guard.

I looked...wrong.

My face was pale, almost grey, my eyes bloodshot and puffy. Sweat clung to my hairline, and my lips were dry and cracked like I hadn't had water in days. I splashed cold water on my face, the shock of it grounding me for a moment. But even that didn't erase the image of the person staring back at me. I barely recognised them.

I didn't know what to do next. Do I tell someone? Who would I even tell? What would I say? "Hey, I think I almost died, but I didn't, and now I feel...weird." That didn't sound right. And even if I did try to explain, who would believe me?

I didn't believe myself.

I shuffled back to my room, every step feeling like a monumental task. I didn't want to think about what just happened, but my mind kept replaying it, over and over, like a broken record. The tightness in my chest, the inability to breathe, the thought that I was dying–it all felt so real.

I lay down on the bed, staring at the ceiling. The fan spun lazily above me, its rhythmic hum the only sound in the room. I tried to focus on it, to let the monotony of its movement distract me, but my thoughts refused to settle.

What was that?

The question lingered in my mind, unanswered. It wasn't just fear. It wasn't just sadness. It was something else entirely—something I didn't have the words for.

I tried to rationalise it. Maybe it was just exhaustion, or maybe I'd eaten something bad. Maybe I was overreacting. But no matter how much I tried to reason with myself, a part of me knew that wasn't true. This wasn't something I could explain away.

This was *new*.

And it scared me.

That night, I didn't sleep. Every time I closed my eyes, I felt the echoes of it creeping back in. My chest would tighten, my breathing would quicken, and I'd jolt awake, heart racing convinced it was happening all over again. I spent the night curled up in bed, clutching my knees to my chest as if that might protect me from whatever was inside me.

Morning came slowly, dragging its feet like it knew I wasn't ready for it. The sunlight poured in through the window, and for a moment, I let myself believe that maybe things would feel normal again. Maybe I could shake it off, pretend it didn't happen, and move on.

But deep down, I knew better.

This was just the beginning.

I just lived those days in somebody else's body. Everything I did felt like a mechanical process, moving through a fog, unconnected to the world around me. My thoughts were screaming at me, cacophonous and impossible to be silenced, but everything else seemed muted, quietened as if the world had just muffled itself for me.

I kept my mouth shut. Not that I didn't want to, but I simply couldn't. The more I tried to articulate those words, the more they got stuck in my throat, lodged somewhere between fear and shame. I told myself that it was nothing, that it was a fluke which would never repeat itself again.

But the fear remained.

It settled in my chest, a constant nagging presence that never went away. It was there, subtle at first, creeping into the edges of my mind when I least expected it. A sudden tightness in my chest when I went out and a strange flutter in my stomach when I heard loud noises.

Then, it became bolder.

I stopped doing things. Little things at first. Stuff like taking phone calls or entering overcrowded rooms. It just felt better to say maybe later, not today, rather than risking it happening again. And those maybe later started turning into never again, and I barely realised my world was shrunk to the size of my room.

It was suffocating, being alone in a way, but worse to be with people. I didn't want to have to explain why I'd jump, why I couldn't sit or why I'd get up in the middle of a conversation without any warning. I couldn't even tell myself why.

And then it happened again.

The second time it happened, I was alone at home again. It started as slow as a whisper, the faint hum of a machine you barely even notice until it is all that is left in your universe. I was sitting at the dining table, mindlessly swiping through my phone, when that familiar leadenness crept over me. My chest seemed tight, like something wrapped itself around me, little by little. But I dismissed it, telling myself it wasn't anything. Maybe I hadn't slept well, or maybe I was just imagining things.

But deep within me, I knew better.

What felt like hours ticked by in minutes. I could feel my heart palpitate fast and loud as each thud echoed into my ears. My palms were wet, and my breathing became shallow, as though I was gasping in a vacuum. At home: a long, long wall, two long, long walls– the ones I'd stared into thousands of times– was suddenly closer, as though pushing in on me; keep telling myself to get going, to do something–is whatever it is–but my legs felt anchored to the floor.

The logical part of my brain fought to take control. You're fine. You're fine. It's nothing. But my body had other plans. Each inhale felt smaller than the last, and suddenly, the air didn't feel enough. My vision blurred at the edges, my head felt light, and there was a sharp, tingling sensation in my fingers and arms, like static electricity buzzing under my skin.

I thought that the first time around, I learned something. I thought I would know what to do if it ever happened again. But at that moment, I felt as helpless as I had before.

The silence was deafening. Every floorboard creaked a little louder, and every outside noise seemed amplified. My mind was running with the terrible thought, What if this is it? What if I die right here, alone, and nobody knows? My head was spinning with worst-case scenarios I couldn't yank myself out of.

I stumbled to my feet, desperate for control, for anything to anchor me to reality. The walls began to blur as I paced the room, my hands trembling as I gripped the edge of the table for support. My phone was right there, within reach, but I couldn't bring myself to pick it up. I didn't know who to call or what to say. "Hey, I think I'm dying, but I'm not sure?"

I tried to do those deep breaths that everyone keeps talking about: breathe in, breathe out, but it felt impossible. Each breath was a fight against the weight crushing my chest. My body had turned against me, working in ways that I could neither predict nor control.

At some point, I don't even know when I found myself on the floor, my back pressed against the cold wall, knees pulled up to my chest. That was the only thing I could do at that moment; I was supposed to keep myself from completely falling apart. I gripped my fists so tight that my nails dug into my palms, the sharp sting grounding me just enough to keep me tethered to the present.

Time didn't feel real anymore. It could've been minutes, it could've been hours–I had no way of knowing. But eventually, the storm inside me began to quiet, little by little. My breaths came easier, though still shaky, and the suffocating tightness in my chest loosened just enough for me to sit up. My body felt drained, like I'd run a marathon without moving an inch.

All of that came to a crashing end when, finally, it was over, leaving me with nothing but my breathing and the hollow echo of what had just been. I sat for such a long time, staring into this empty room, weighed by the feeling of how awful it must be to experience all of this alone.

I didn't cry. Not that I wanted not to, but I couldn't. It was like I had spent all the emotion I had; now, there was only numbness. As I sat there, trying to pick the pieces of myself up off the floor, there was one thought that kept repeating over and over in my mind: What if it happens again?

As I sat there on that cold, cold floor that day, wholly drained and depleted of all the energy and vitality but with some hollow, lingering ache to it, profound exhaustion, something that I had been holding back and avoiding for too long, that moment was significant in realising it to me.

This experience of mine was not only one related to the situation surrounding me; it wasn't just about the paralysing anxiety or a tight grip of panic over myself, nor was it exactly about the distressing fact that my own body started morphing into a tremendous battlefield, full of fierce conflicts. No, that was everything–the deep scarring I had had up throughout my life, painful scars that I had hidden so skillfully that I almost succeeded in convincing myself that they just did not exist, never really affecting me.

Every single memory, every single moment that I had desperately tried to bury deep within myself, somehow managed to claw its way back to the very surface of my consciousness. And with every assault from these intrusive thoughts, it felt as if those moments were insisting, almost demanding, to be felt deeply, acknowledged fully, and faced head-on without any further avoidance.

I hated it.

I loathed how utterly powerless it made me feel, and I detested how vulnerable and exposed it left me in such a raw state. But, sitting there, looking out into the desolate emptiness surrounding me in that space, I could not help but think of the hard fact settling into my mind that this was a situation that would not evaporate. This was something with which I was not going to escape. However much my fervent attempts at getting out of this may seem to be, no matter how intense these may seem to be.

It's just very peculiar, isn't it? How something that you cannot even see with your eyes can break you and destroy you this far? How, suddenly, something as simple and instinctive as breathing, something you have done effortlessly for your entire existence without a second thought, suddenly becomes the impossible challenge in front of you, like breathing might be impossible to do sometimes. And probably the saddest part about all of this is that nobody around you ever really perceives what you are doing. No one knows of the struggle going on inside you –unless, of course, you reveal it to them, and even when you do, they still can't feel how deeply you are experiencing this.

I desperately hope sincerely to be able to say that at that point, I somehow found a solution or perhaps an enlightened epiphany that would make it all so much better. Well, the reality is life does not seem to get worked out in this neat, simple way, and neither am I someone who fits into the mould.

At that specific point in time, all that I knew was the oppressive feeling of how tired I was– tired of constantly fighting that has to take place each day, of putting on this pretentious air of being fine, and just tired of carrying everything around me, without any kind of help or support.

Beneath all of this overwhelming sense of weariness, however, some small part of me clung tenaciously to a glimmer of hope, a will to keep moving and just get on with it. Perhaps it's not because I wanted to, but because I had to.

Because isn't that really what life is all about? It is, after all, a complex series of moments—some of which have the power to break you down and leave you feeling shattered, while others serve to build you up and reinforce your strength. Most of these moments, however, seem to leave you in a state of limbo, somewhere suspended in between those extremes.

And perhaps, just maybe, the essence of life isn't primarily focused on uncovering answers or seeking out solutions to all of our problems. Maybe, in the grand scheme of things, it's really more about enduring and surviving through the various moments that threaten to completely unravel you.

As I stood up from that floor, my legs shaking but steady enough to hold me, I didn't feel victorious. I didn't feel strong. But I felt alive. And for now, that was enough.

This book is not about resolutions or the traditional story of how things get all wrapped up nicely. It does not bother itself with the idea of loose ends being tied up, nor does it bother to find some happy ending that ties everything together so perfectly. Instead, it chronicles my personal life, an examination of my journey, the scars I carry, and the major events that have played a pivotal role in shaping me into who I am today. It brings light to all the different battles I have been in throughout my life, battles I have fought valiantly and lost and the ones I am still actively fighting each day.

Perhaps in all of this, I've learned to find some semblance of understanding in the midst of chaos, not necessarily for anyone's benefit but primarily for mine. For, when we think of it, that is all we can truly do, is it? We gather pieces of our brokenness and attempt to construct something meaningful out of them.

So, here I am, at this moment, presenting to you the fragments of my being, the narrative that encapsulates my journey. I am not sharing this with you because it is something extraordinary or remarkable but because it holds significance as it is uniquely mine. And if you have managed to journey this far alongside me, then perhaps, in some meaningful way, it has also become a part of your experience.

As I walked out of that room, I left behind a deep silence, the feeling as if it would have been an even heftier blanket wrapped around my entire self. Parts of myself I had grown tired of lugging far longer than I had the time for lingered inside because of this moment. Sunset elegantly into the horizon outside. Oranges and purples above, as they danced into the sky, were something wonderful. In this moment, I finally breathed in, unrequired nor forced.

And that was how the day ended.

Final Thoughts

Life is a series of contradictions, a constant dance between what we crave and fear. I have spent so much time trying to make sense of these opposing forces, trying to untangle the web of emotions that tightens with every choice, every mistake, and every fleeting moment of joy.

Joy.

It is a word that feels too simple for what it represents. When it comes, it takes everything and sweeps you into a state where nothing else matters.

But for me, joy has always been a double-edged sword. It's a fleeting visitor that leaves behind an unshakable emptiness, a haunting clarity that strips everything down to its raw, uncomfortable truth.

When I get overindulgent, it's like a switch flips. That thing that felt good a moment before is now a point of regret. Every choice I made to attain that moment of happiness is wrong, misplaced, and even foolish.

It's not only the joy that I am thinking about; it's the fact that I gave in to the feeling itself. Even my very existence starts to feel heavy, like a burden I chose to carry without realizing its weight.

And then I wonder if, in the future, I may regret the very decision to publish this book.

At this moment, it feels like a triumph: a testament to everything I've lived through, everything I've poured out onto these pages. But what if later I question whether it was worth it?

Was it worth exposing parts of myself, letting my vulnerabilities out in the open? What if that weight, too, is something I wish I could undo?

It's a weird cycle of regret and clarity, always questioning whether the choices I make at my most honest are ones I am prepared to live with. Or maybe that's just how I am, looking back with a lens that feels sharper than it might have to be.

About the Author-

I am Sankalpit Salaria, and this book is a reflection of my struggle, growth, and everything in between. Growing up in a desi household, I was taught very early on about the unspoken battles that many teens go through: loneliness, emotional turmoil, and the pressure of societal expectations. It has been a shaping journey for me, and it shapes the way I look at the world, I hope through my writing, I will be able to connect with others who may feel the same way.

"Through the Darkened Glass" is my first book, in which I talk about abandonment, self-discovery, and the complexity of human emotions. I attempt to describe the silent struggles that many of us face but rarely talk about. I hope this book gives readers a sense of understanding and empathy, making them feel a little less alone in their journeys.

When I am not writing, I am reflecting, observing, and looking for inspiration in the world around me. So, this book is the beginning of a very long journey of being a writer, and I am excited to share more stories with you.

Acknowledgements

This book wouldn't have happened without the incredible support from my friends, online and offline. What began as personal journaling turned out to be something much bigger when I shared it with them. They didn't just listen to my words; they believed in them. They saw potential in me that I couldn't see myself, and it was that belief that encouraged me to take the leap and turn my writing into a book.

To my friends, near and far, who have encouraged me and reminded me of the strength in my words–thank you. Your steady support instilled in me the confidence to persevere, and for that, I am deeply grateful.